THE PORTAGE POETRY SERIES

Series Titles

Let It Be Told in a Single Breath
Russell Thorburn

The Blue Divide
Linda Nemec Foster

Lake, River, Mountain
Mark B. Hamilton

The Watching Sky
Judy Brackett Crowe

Poetic People Power
Tara Bracco (ed.)

Talking Diamonds
Linda Nemec Foster

The Green Vault Heist
David Salner

There is a Corner of Someplace Else
Camden Michael Jones

Everything Waits
Jonathan Graham

We Are Reckless
Christy Prahl

Always a Body
Molly Fuller

Bowed As If Laden With Snow
Megan Wildhood

Silent Letter
Gail Hanlon

New Wilderness
Jenifer DeBellis

Fulgurite
Catherine Kyle

The Body Is Burden and Delight
Sharon White

Bone Country
Linda Nemec Foster

Not Just the Fire
R.B. Simon

Monarch
Heather Bourbeau

The Walk to Cefalù
Lynne Viti

The Found Object Imagines a Life: New and Selected Poems
Mary Catherine Harper

Naming the Ghost
Emily Hockaday

Mourning
Dokubo Melford Goodhead

Messengers of the Gods: New and Selected Poems
Kathryn Gahl

After the 8-Ball
Colleen Alles

Careful Cartography
Devon Bohm

Broken On the Wheel
Barbara Costas-Biggs

Sparks and Disperses
Cathleen Cohen

Holding My Selves Together: New and Selected Poems
Margaret Rozga

Lost and Found Departments
Heather Dubrow

Marginal Notes
Alfonso Brezmes

The Almost-Children
Cassondra Windwalker

Meditations of a Beast
Kristine Ong Muslim

Praise for

Let It Be Told in a Single Breath

"Only Russell Thorburn could have written this book, which is the greatest attribute of any book. What Thorburn brings to his subject matter moves beyond knowing and bleeds over into a way of seeing and saying and breathing. When I need to know who else in the world is feeling alive in the moment and nostalgic about the past and who wishes to celebrate those who've come before us, I know I can always turn to the poems of Russell Thorburn to make me believe that poetry does indeed matter, that it is still a living breathing way of being in the world."

—Peter Markus
author of *When Our Fathers Return to Us as Birds*

"More than any living poet I know, Russell Thorburn invites us into the company of recurring characters inhabiting a fully-formed world of the imagination. His work reads, collectively, like a vast, ongoing novel in which we join personalities from John Keats to John Lennon to Marilyn Monroe and get to discover what they are up to these days. In this new book, for example, I was delighted to learn that Keats and his gal Fanny are hiding out in the cold north, safe in an old hotel overlooking Lake Superior. And Thorburn and his readers get to play too, as he has the generosity and talent to write himself and us into this irresistible poetic Elysium (and sometimes Underworld) of his."

—Jonathan Johnson
author of *May Is an Island*

"Oh, the images that become coals within our memory. One thing I love: these poems protect the sensual phenomenology of love's reveries. As John Prine would say, these poems are more like souvenirs. Each is presented and bathed within a threshold where life became...what? Maybe where life became alive."

—Ken Meisel
author of *The Light Most Glad of All*

"Anachronistic poems comprise the best in Russell Thorburn's new collection, *Let It Be Told in a Single Breath*. With titles that elicit chuckles, making what follows irresistible ('John Keats One Evening Beheld Lake Superior'), we easily slip into narratives whose rhetoric turns on the unexpected. Particularly delightful are Russell Thorburn's iconic depiction of character, surprise settings, and signature costuming. To wit: 'After his stew of suckling pig, slow cooked /in a red-wine sauce,' Jim Harrison greets the poet Lorca at his door. One night, Richard Brautigan and his hippie girlfriend arrive at a service station in the Upper Peninsula. Dressed in black, Edgar Allan Poe is back, 'The collar of [his] wrinkled shirt up around /his bird neck . . . his mustache unwieldy.' Elsewhere in the book, lyrical poems about the poet's wife resonate deeply. In other pieces, most light and like cuts from film, appear Guillaume Apollinaire, Jack Kerouac, Billy the Kid, Charles Bukowski, Bob Dylan, Marvin Gaye, John Lennon, Marilyn Monroe, Sugar Baby, and others. This brilliant book immerses us in the impassioned memories of Russell Thorburn, shaped by the Civil Rights Movement, the Vietnam War, Motown music, world poets, sports heroes, and other legendary figures."

—Beverly Matherne
author of *Love Potions, Teas, Incantations*
U.P. Poet Laureate (MI), 2023 & 2024

"There is a genuine earthiness to the imagistic and engaging narrative poems of Russell Thorburn. Russ is one of Michigan's best known and widely respected poets from southern Michigan to the far northern reaches of its Upper Peninsula. There is much news to get from his poems that cover a wide range of topics from rock 'n' roll history to beat poets to the beauty of glorious nature in Michigan and beyond. Russell Thorburn is a poet I love to read, and you'll be glad to meet his finely crafted words on the page that will continue to feed your soul."

—M. L. Liebler
author of *I Want to Be Once*
co-editor of *Respect: The Poetry of Detroit Music*

"The far ranging, complex poems in Thorburn's *Let It Be Told in a Single Breath* emerge from the page with heart and build to fever, into and out of dislocations in time, place, memory, insight. I couldn't help myself but to keep leaning in to catch hold of the voices from the page. 'When we turned over in our dreams / we found each other standing there together…and like all dreams / they end before they have begun.' Indeed, and too soon."

—M. Bartley Seigel
author of *This Is What They Say*
U.P. Poet Laureate (MI), 2021–22
Academy of American Poets Laureate Fellow

"Russell Thorburn's *Let It Be Told in a Single Breath* adds to his rich, intimate body of evocative writing. Reading this new collection is like meeting an old friend you haven't seen for a while—you pick up right where you left off. Though even if you are new to Thorburn's work, you too will soon feel like an old friend. From the shores of Lake Superior to the city streets of Detroit, he's been there and he's seen things, and his wistful wisdom takes us down a lot of literal and figurative roads. A poet of praise and of lament, Thorburn personalizes even the most iconic figures of literature, music, sports, and popular culture while in the process of creating new myths and legends."

—Jim Daniels
author of *The Middle Ages*

"In *Let It Be Told in a Single Breath*, Russell Thorburn pays tribute to the musical luminaries of his generation. Thorburn transcends the trite fanfare typically reserved for writing that takes rock music as its theme and finds the plaintive notes and harsher realities of aesthetic beauty. In this book, we find a highly-skilled, musical poet in a high-level conversation full of mirth and sadness. The vision here is Keatsian in its complex figurations of beauty. The poems will break your heart while affirming your faith in the timeless power of music."

—Cal Freeman
author of *Poolside at the Dearborn Inn*

"Courtyard Balladeers" © Steven White, inspired by the poem "The Last Place on Earth in Mexico City." The blind guitarist accompanies an accordionist in his Mexico City repair shop. The sign above them in Spanish announces "repairmen."

LET IT BE TOLD IN A SINGLE BREATH

POEMS

RUSSELL THORBURN

CORNERSTONE PRESS
UNIVERSITY OF WISCONSIN-STEVENS POINT

Cornerstone Press, Stevens Point, Wisconsin 54481
Copyright © 2024 Russell Thorburn
www.uwsp.edu/cornerstone

Printed in the United States of America by
Point Print and Design Studio, Stevens Point, Wisconsin

Library of Congress Control Number: 2023945133
ISBN: 978-1-960329-17-2

Cornerstone Press titles are produced in courses and internships offered by the
Department of English at the University of Wisconsin–Stevens Point.

DIRECTOR & PUBLISHER
Dr. Ross K. Tangedal

EXECUTIVE EDITORS
Jeff Snowbarger, Fressia McKee

EDITORIAL DIRECTOR
Ellie Atkinson

SENIOR EDITORS
Brett Hill, Grace Dahl

PRESS STAFF
Carolyn Czerwinski, Zoie Dinehart, Kirsten Faulkner, Natalie Reiter, Lauren Rudesill,
Anthony Thiel

For my bright star, Emily

Bright star, would I were stedfast as thou art—
Not in lone splendour hung aloft the night
And watching, with eternal lids apart,
Like nature's patient, sleepless Eremite,
The moving waters at their priestlike task
Of pure ablution round earth's human shores

—John Keats

Also by Russell Thorburn:

Somewhere We'll Leave the World

Misfit Hearts

The Whole Tree as Told to the Backyard

The Drunken Piano

Father, Tell Me I Have Not Aged

The Weight of Umber and Sienna

Approximate Desire

CONTENTS

— I —

— II —

— III —

— IV —

— I —

Love Song with Boreal Forest

Let these shoes speak of running through snow
to reach her name buried in the woods,

her face imperfectly freckled and her blouse
unbuttoned in all its soft thoughts of him;

in love with his own voice and that of his muse
whose eyebrows are temporary nests of the beautiful.

Brown scuffed-up hiking shoes, dumb beasts
who don't know when to stay home and dry,

they know everything about him, where
he's running to and where he's run from

before meeting her, how he once stood shivering
as a boy on the road wandering anywhere;

and now he waits for her eyebrows to tighten
into this thin antenna, for her cheekbones

to widen, like always in this dream that pours
from his insomnia in the key of G minor,

perhaps his favorite of all the darker sounds
for his shoes to saunter on ahead

of the lazy pattern on the keyboard;
his coat laid open by her curious fingers,

each button a trail back to her: his lover
moving in the old ways to relearn his presence;

breathing his name slowly, she shifts her large
hips in a diminished chord, the quiet unlike

any silence he has heard before. Seeing
him again, she looks for something forgotten

in an old drawer pulled out of her antique dresser;
her regret wears no lacy nightgown,

as if it were mythological and not real;
their love of flesh leaves behind the bitterness

in the tiny bed of a mattress on a floor, while
he removes his shoes, and all of his wet clothes.

Her eyes follow the line of his thigh,
then his shoulders the color of winter.

There, in his body, lies the remembered delight,
the heart's argument against loneliness.

Wandering the Yellow Dog

Jim Harrison wrote of the Russian poet,
Yesenin, who hanged himself after writing
his last poem in blood. Harrison was in debt,
unpublished, living on a hardscrabble farm
in northern Michigan, and back from Leningrad.
Everything's so fragile except ropes, noted
the poet once, who now tightens a noose
from moonlight and wears it round his neck
in my dream of him, like gray paraffin.
A little more than seventy, he hobbles,
using a cane to test spongy ground,
skirting the blueness of a rivulet
as it curves through heavy grassland.
He stoops for a black-capped mushroom,
his dream beard unshaven and unseemly,
like his one eye looking on faithfully
for any image that takes him to the far corners
of a sky drenched in an impossible blueness.
And the old poet wanders into Mulligan Creek,
wading with blue-bottled flies, like sipping
good vodka for a second, his feet
sunk down into this wine of song,
waiting for a buzz to float away.
His deeply wrinkled face looks for what
can never change from that canvas
of blue, and he knows he will die
and no longer tread the earth
as he wades deeper into the clear creek.

Drinking with Jim Harrison at the Hotel Bar

It was Harrison at a bar decades ago
who spoke to me about Malcolm Lowry,
his unfinished novel high on our list
for reading that winter but who reads
that mad genius today other than alcoholics
or poets wanting a close look inside.
To be alone is to be alive, Harrison said,
inferring that to get inside the soul
as it was called you had to pick desolate
places of snow or shine. His grisly face
of a one-eyed Inuit sage was overburdened
by death, that coin which was flipped
up in the air many times to see if he'd live
or die when it landed: heads or tails.
Whenever we looked outside at the snow,
an eyelid of his appeared to twitch,
veins widened in his vast forehead.
He ordered one vodka after another
at the hotel bar where I was a night porter
not exactly on the job or doing anything,
the two of us suddenly throwing back drinks.
I was working to support three sons and wife,
our house of over one hundred years.
If I told Harrison this, I don't know,
and after so many drinks, I'd be on
the blacklist for working there without
the enthusiasm of somebody on his way
to the scaffold: that noose Harrison
knew in his Yesenin letters. Everybody
got fired at the hotel. I was one. But only
a few got to meet with Harrison whose
way of talking was a kind of percussion.

You never heard such beats of resolute silences,
his mind among the dragonflies and mosquitoes
where he'd sing of a girl with freckles
and eyes like a sky that seemed to last forever
as long as he kept talking, as long as he kept moving
toward something he knew would never be there again.

Richard Manuel Crashes His Cadillac

His world speaks to him through the windshield:
one crack dividing his before and after
of alcohol consumption and love for a woman.
The deer caught in his headlights turns to say
you can kill me if you want, but I am not going to move.
Its head turned up for the crash
and Richard Manuel sees not a deer now
but a wife who got away through the woods
troubled by his drinking and nights across the line.
Jane, he cries out as if he could warn her
before his chrome dented from accidents
collides with her thoughtful body.
Her name can't save him from the crash
on this mountainside and he sees it almost
in slow motion now, into the deer, then veering
off the road and a splintering thud.
He listens to the radiator hissing. Touching his mouth
that hit the rearview mirror, he sees his fingers
are the color of blackberries in the dim interior light.
He closes his eyes for a minute to feel
the earth spinning through the snowy whispers,
speaks the names Paula and Joshua,
his children, as if to slow that last revolution.
Tearing off his coat, he slides from his seat
to walk the cold mist and as above
a moon drives careful of the many stars.

They Really Make a Mess Outta You

—from "Just Like Tom Thumb's Blues"

Maybe this isn't the place to say it, but like Dylan
I love watching the Three Stooges: Moe
with his finger ready to solve any trouble
with a quick eye-poke, his face frosted with pie
that descended like a prophecy; Larry
with his wild poet's hair waiting for the wisecrack
to break like an egg and yoke the cheeks and chin.

Larry who mouths absurdity and is rewarded
with a kick in the ass, and, finally, Curly
because he is my favorite crunching egg shells
for breakfast in that hunger of odd man out;
his tiny bow tie eating his neck, and that galloping
charge when he is mad enough to take on Moe.
I don't think they ever thought about dying,
or if a flying finger could blind them.

They are my secret pleasure, a link to my childhood
when I ate pancakes and watched the Three Stooges
in a golden age of mayhem, their pratfalls
accompanied by a verbal schizophrenia.
Here I am, sixty years old, ready for more Stooges:
the Lady Godiva episode and my first shiver
of sexuality, or the liquid fireworks from the Stooges
digging up a high-society lawn and bursting water pipes.
I don't want to ever lose my love for slapstick—
a sunrise without sweet violence would kill me.

Moe with his head caught in armor, Larry
posing like a millennium poet with his hair in chaos be-

fore a transcendent scramble through a wax museum
to escape the ape—Curly bouncing his belly off
the gorilla, head down in uncontrollable rage.
We never grow old if we laugh, murder language
with Curly, marvel at "cer-tain-ly," delivered
skin-headed and deadpan from his barreled mouth,
later to be borrowed by Dylan for the purring
snarl of his own lament.

Dead Poets Who Visit Jim Harrison

After his stew of suckling pig, slow cooked
in a red-wine sauce, his one eye of an Inuit hunter
observes through his window of deceit
the dead poet Lorca coming back.
Seventy-some-years old, Jim Harrison,
not wearing a shirt and underwear,
with his cock unfettered, downs
one more vodka, his beloved Stolichnaya.
He watches Federico stop at his door,
as if looking for those loves he won't ever meet again.
Tapping on the double-glazed window
to get the poet's attention, he lifts his vodka
bottle up for all dead poets to drink.
His blood's gorged on cheese, desserts,
beluga spooned from a half-pound jar.
He didn't live alone in Patagonia but more
than anybody he understood how to die.
A dead bird falls from the roof. One more
casualty of the heat. And the articulate desert
wind plays on its five-stringed guitar.
Letters from his editor balled up on the floor,
a cluttered desk of greasy plates and cheese
wheels that have rolled on inside his gut:
Pacifico beer bottles empty like late October.
Back in Montana he wrote on a yellow page
it's zero and 80 mph winds. Now he's pouring Lorca
his first drink from a coffee cup with coffee
still in it, and talking about hot southern sands
yearning for white camellias. A rattlesnake
that bit his favorite dog he had to shoot.
Come on in, Jim says, knowing Yesenin
somewhere in the yard waits with his rope.

Break from the Bus Ride: Convenience Store on US-2

After two a.m. on the bus headed toward the Mackinac Bridge,
I watch the prisoner who, for the first time in years,
strolls among the junk food; his troubled eyes show no trace
of murder. Like me he has miles to travel on this bus to Saginaw,
rolling on through the night buried in yesterday's snow.

I was traveling cheap, out of work, a poet of forty
following the inmate through the store.
I heard his cold hallelujah leave his sour breath:
all journeys are the same but he wasn't singing,
this black man from the walled castle.
Like Roethke I taught men like him poetry, who twisted space
with speech in their cell, wrestling with conscience.

Before boarding the bus in Marquette, a prison guard
leaned into his shoulder and muttered something
in the tight cage of his ear that made him cringe.
He walked the aisles, buying nothing.
I looked closely when he was about to pocket
a Milky Way for old time's sake; dance a step ten years
old; gaze up at the surveillance camera, daring it
to play back his most guarded secrets.

He gave the finger to the moving lens, and I thought
of him as Macbeth from a prison play, his voice powerful
as that cursed king who made bones out of his freedom
after throwing his life away in a fading dream.

The Sweet Loneliness of Solitary Travel

Charlene was what Joni Mitchell called herself
riding home to California on Interstate 10,

red-wigged and sunglassed, for the drifter
she had become. No driver's license, the folkie

from Alberta, Canada, knew the truckers
during the day would signal her white Mercedes

of the presence of marauding cop cars:
she got to know some of these American truckers

along Mobile, Gulfport, New Orleans,
stopping for coffee and blue plate specials,

after that tarmac of endless cars, truck stops
and motel rooms; her name was Charlene,

a fictional dreamer of the road who sought escape
from tours and boyfriends: she sang of the clouds

of Michelangelo, what the road said to her
while she ascertained where she was westbound

and taking refuge in the roads
those thundering heart bass chords.

Waitresses told her more of the road,
of truckers with heartache in their rearview

love affairs, who brought their miles while waitresses
on tired legs served them smiling eggs,

busty laughter, a joke or two during coffee
refills. They donned their own secret lives,

left children with strangers to watch,
bruises from mayhem in their love liaisons,

and Charlene knew her poetry wound
around the loneliness of a curve,

an oil rig pumping into the motherland
those hips of the earth she careened past.

What was left of last night's dream,
the cars as sets of waves,

she told her beehived server, before
handing her so many dollar bills.

Her life a travelogue of beach towns
and highway hand-me-downs,

she adjusted that red wig, sunglasses
taken off the table to say goodbye

as a stranger in a diner, never arriving,
only leaving something behind.

Lost: A Love Poem for Emily

We pass that road sign with buckshot,
cars riding over the centerline
about to damage us but never do
with drunken headlights and brutal metal.
My wife, I know, will forgive me
for saying our exit was the next one
when it wasn't. Upon exiting we were lost.

This lostness lasts like the sky washed blue,
roads without signage of where we were,
while we rode past cattails and wetlands,
wondering which road would take us to our son's.
We laughed nervously at the water tower
with the name of his town, Verona,
but crossed borders without getting anywhere,
us circling it too many times to know better.

This constant for us to note while
we were lost, and she spoke of the water tower
as a sort of constellation in the night sky.
Soon it will be dark without finding our road.
I saw the fields revolve through her hair,
midnight strands that swallow the gray,
her almost slender body beside me,
the same as it was at nineteen.

In a while we're talking about simple things,
like birdlife, the squawkers and mockers
who populate the dusty light of evening.
How many deer that we will see on this trip
to visit our son. Her lips speak to me
of mountains, of the gathering cold
when we roll down windows for fresh air,
of the love flooding our lives still.

On the Bus Downtown along Woodward Avenue
the Driver Turns around to Say They Killed Marvin Gaye

Not much of Woodward is visible
when the ice-battered bus spins its tires
and the driver thinks he could be long gone,

as he slides across the frozen road,
bumping against three smaller vehicles
with commuters cursing their morning schedules.

Marcellus, the stubbled-cheek driver,
manages to shout around his shoulder
at the presence of a black man,

older than yesterday, yellowed teeth,
hair like roots of plants growing
out of his nose, announcing that the radio

doesn't play good tunes, as if suddenly
it was his fault, that fifty-something worker
in a ragged coat off to nowhere

but the end of the line. "What about Marvin Gaye?"
he asks, one eye on the storm
that wants to ice his windshield.

This morning his wife in curlers
saw a tired man that looked like Marvin Gaye
pulling on his trousers worn through the bottom.

His heart gone soft and blue, he stares
out his window of a bus frosted over with snow
and the cold hard hands of winter.

The driver holds on tight to the steering wheel
that turns them around the Ford Pinto
dead on the road, and he's singing to those

who've taken this morning a seat
on the downtown bus. "And I'll be doggone
if you ain't warm as a breath of spring."

A woman with the white, fiery hair
of an oracle, her pillbox hat from another era,
hangs onto the rope that buzzes the next stop.

But Marcellus ignores that hanging
when the woman mumbles, "Why ain't you slowing
down?" as they go skidding sideways through

an intersection, her hand still clenched
to the rope passing those waiting for the bus,
and he won't stop singing Marvin Gaye;

won't stop the freeway from tempting him
to swerve off the avenue and abandon
this job as a bus driver forever.

Sergeant Reese Pummels Sugar Baby in the Ring

In his gloves letting everything go, his curses,
these blood oaths, damaging as his punches.
Now one more Manhattan and his gums
bleed. Reese's mouth is but a mumble of boxing dreams.
A couple dances to no music, an overweight blonde
who dyed her roots and the sober-faced man called Lucky.
For no luck at all, six years in jail for being wrongly
accused. Next to the boxer sits his friend Kojak,
lending a hand if he wants to use the urinal,
or to stand lost in thought over the girl
back in Baghdad. Sergeant Reese armored
and on patrol, and not thinking of death
for several seconds when their eyes meet, the girl
who defies religion in a single blonde curl,
her espresso lifted slowly, teasingly to her lips.
He looks for her in the crowd at the bar,
a nineteen-year-old dangerous to love.
Her life contained in a heap of hijab blowing
around her in the heat. He sees the danger
as intoxicating, with the dancing couple's hips
buried in a song, her hive of hair abuzz against his chest.
Then the beat dissolves into hot white acid of shouting rap.
His brother counted along with the referee
the first time Reese fell to the ring—they ride
in that Humvee to the desert's edge
looking for killers. Reese tells Kojak
he loved that girl in the café and he was going
to marry her, despite the sand of absence
drifting everywhere. But in the bar,
knowing they looked for something they couldn't
name or hold close before it killed them,
these gladiators stagger up from their seats.

Something about Eighteen and Goose Lake Festival Where I Saw the Flying Burrito Brothers Play

Dreaming of ten thousand places
we weren't supposed to be, we became jumpers
of wire fences, fooling soft equivalents
of the Hells Angels when we rode
the mesh and dropped over the top.
I looked at the pot-bellied long hairs
in motorcycle jackets, bandaged bruises
wanting to be free of bad skin but not this weekend.
With thick-maned hair we wandered
a year after Woodstock, through the cropped crowd,
who sprawled on beach blankets
in a pasture of blistering heat.

We had left the planet, one with wire
protecting us from such scenes, and I saw Gram Parsons
alive as he could be, up on stage wearing
his nudie duds with the Flying Burrito Brothers,
whose pencil-thin mustache was barely grown in.
This old town is filled with sin,
Gram sang to the crowd, waving his hips
like hands at the sunburned faces of girls, whose
pill taking would keep them from making thirty;
on guitar his man played pedal steel, unburdening a sound
like streams of wire waving end on end.

We were jumpers with fences inside us, too.
Like Gram who couldn't find a last handhold
to pull him free before so many stars settled in his lungs.
We strolled past fences that kept us
contained like cattle, some with blown bits
of newspaper, or other daylong debris.

We assembled in lines for outhouse troughs,
a part of the dreaming people, who had come
for what could no longer be explained, saw stars
at night like those drafted soldiers who never
escaped their bloody fate in Vietnam to dream
of other places they had never been at eighteen.

Willie Horton Dressed in his Baseball Uniform, after Playing the Yankees at Tiger Stadium

His home run lifted up over the fence
to beat the Yankees in the second game
of a doubleheader that afternoon,
but the rioters won't listen to him standing
on top of his Cadillac, the men who burn
storefronts, brick their weapons against
the National Guard. Willie with his number
23 on his baseball jersey crying out, "Don't burn up
your own starlight, brothers, be left with no shine
here in the Motor City." He grew up on 12th Street
and Clairmount, and in their faces sees his own
who at sixteen hit his first home run at Tiger Stadium
playing for a high school team. His bat would
club them to the World Series next year,
his compact power visible in his body,
as he sways on top of his luxury car. Not knowing
which way to go, he yells, "Don't steal that television."
The Tiger left fielder watches these flames
exhaust their fuel and spiral upward into smoke
above the city: a blessing for him to be there
with nobody heeding his words; learning what's
wrong rooted deep under their words. It was easier
for him to pull his heavy bat in to his body
and demolish the next Yankee pitch, the winning
pitcher John Hiller after Podres tired in the fourth
and he came on to face Yankee batters for the fifth
and sixth. But none of the rioters want to hear
the box score, busy carting away TV sets and furniture,
like refugees on the street under the scrutiny
of helicopters and guardsmen in trucks.

Horton hears the injustice crackle like flames
consuming the buildings, gunshots aimed
at both rioters and guardsmen, and he slowly
climbs down from his car, knowing he has struck out.
His neighbors line up around him, here's Willie, they say,
but Detroit doesn't care for baseball as much as the little
girl who won't eat her sandwich, the tired factory man
who aims for home after hours of working a job
that tastes like sulfur and eats out his lungs from cleaning
out the foundry with a wiry weeping broom.

In Winter Park, Florida, after Playing Their Final Set at the Cheek to Cheek Lounge

Levon shook his head at Richard Manuel
sitting on the bed in the motel room.
His voice had never cracked so badly,
while trying to sing his falsetto,
"We carried you in our arms on Independence Day."
His piano chords stacked on top of one
another like a mansion under his fingers,
and with the amplifiers still buzzing,
Manuel knew a song's true structure
was built from somewhere in the edges
where the words never fit.

After their return to roots,
Robbie said this was where he got off,
his body wasted from touring, the next cigarette
always worse than the one before when
every road led to the same lonely place.
Manuel threw his cigarette at the TV,
the late-night news all bad,
and he walked past Levon, out the door
to his motel room, head down
a mop of black hair hiding despair
at having sunk so low; he didn't care
for anyone to see him, as he chugged his Grand Marnier
and the shower curtain fluttered.

Manuel stepped into the stall,
knowing his voice was second-rate now
as the circuit they'd been playing for years,
but standing on the ledge he let
acoustics from this small, most-private room

help him hit the final high note,
looped his belt tight about his neck,
weight bending the curtain rod,
leaving his bandmates minutes later,
drowning in the moonlight, to carry
him into the parking lot on this,
his Independence Day.

A Last Picnic

It takes her effort to climb, springing legs
up on a sheep rock, his wife like a colossal
shell-trekking tortoise slow before the moon
crashes down on them. She lowers her shoulders
to observe each step, her forehead bathed in gold light.
Her wide, almost laughing skirt in a circus
of strong hips, shifting breasts in their trampoline bounce.
The low, crouching stance of mountains talks
about eternity. She puffs past her husband,
out of breath for a middle-aged lady, a picnic basket
with wine bottles poking out from the wicker,
as he breathes in the bible of her body, soiled knees
from wedging hands for grips to pull her across volcanic rock,
the dusting of other thoughts sprinkled like snow.
Inside the dome of crackling gray light, their
feet lose their footing; to reach the pinnacle
they drag themselves along, his mouth smothered
in a rib-breaking hack and his lady's brow sweating.
Settled down now, his blue-gray eyes narrow
on her shaking out tablecloths, her wifely fingers
spreading mustard on thickly sliced Swiss cheese bread,
and she manages to open a bottle for them,
her Italian sunhat removed for a night wind
in its gentleness rustling their linen jackets.
Her wrinkles are nothing at forty.
Coughing again from exertion, he feels
much older than her, and in great deliberation
he lifts his slender arms to remove his coat,
and struggles to impart a laugh like a little scream.

Billy the Kid in the Lava Tube

Far from New Mexico and familiar brown faces,
Billy the Kid crawled into the hole
and stood up for a hidden photo
in the cathedral light of the lava tube
here in the Mojave. The roots of the earth
above funneled a soulful glow around
his young unshaven beard bristling
from almost golden light. Billy the Kid,
fearful of corners, nowhere to escape,
a buck-toothed killer, knew the sloping
bare backs of women, as he did
the drumbeat tight rocks of the arroyo,
and the tom-toms of the beating down sun.
Again he heard the silence in the hole
known as a hideout by those on the run.
His smile hardened like old bread,
but the hole was for a photograph,
a safe place to pass into legend,
his usually busy hands clasping a rifle.
The hooded man asked him not to move,
told Billy it'd be good for him to be underground
and to pose with death poking from a pocket
of his chapped jacket; squinting bloodshot eyes,
he checked for sidewinders, their rattling deity.
One bite would open heaven.

My Dreams Never Caught Their Bus

I looked into the mirror and saw an older man
staring back in the image of Captain Beefheart
when he played at a ballroom in Detroit
and walked onstage before the Kinks
wearing his crushed hello of a hat down over ears.
I was younger then without crow's feet
and mottled nose, hairs riding the dirty shells
of my ears. Dreams were shot with quick camera
work for a young man in his twenties trying
to wake up before it was late afternoon
and that pillow where my boyhood lay
became a drug to forget the draft.
The silence in the house like a museum
for my last days on earth. But that never
came despite my trying to kill myself
with a handful of sleeping pills.
Dreams burned like Viking boats
out in a mysterious harbor somewhere
and the war crept close on television.
The curly dark tangled hair of a woman
on shore beckoned before the dream channel
changed and there was Captain Beefheart.
I had never given him any thought until
that loss of hair and a bolder brow showed.
These dreams never caught their bus
and left me standing before the mirror
where I mused over his verbose mustache
above that movable upper lip,
unable to get a break in becoming a poet.

When We Lived at the Old Hotel

We were guilty of our hot plate blowing
the hotel fuse, forcing the cook in his pill of a hat
to come down to our room bearing fuses.
One door down roomed Mister Marshall,
who, we were sure, ate out every night.
The elderly guest wore a fedora cocked
slightly to one side like Sinatra.
In his room cramped and lonely as ours, we must
have interfered with his TV shows
when we collapsed in our bed
for that fire and softness, her body often posing
in a mirror first, wide-hipped and curvy, with
her rich walnut-brown hair and aquiline nose.
I wanted to write love poems for her,
my typewriter too loud for the old hotel;
she was my beautiful model with her
unending wave of curls and freckles.
But my handwriting was as hard to read
as a late-night blizzard. On the sixth floor,
we ate rice dishes at the restaurant,
and sipped coffee, and talked as if in a play.
Love was left for the way we braided words
in conversation, our eye contact continuous,
and I liked to say her name that first year we were in love.
Emily, a gentle name that sounded like poetry
and needed my yellow pad, a pencil to catch
the passion for her shapely legs, her belly rounded
like this drum that beat when we touched.
At the library visible from a window,
the ledge where we kept our milk, my fingers
danced across the portable Smith Corona, often
misspelling her name in heavy black strikes of the keys:
Eimly, Eimly, Eimly, over and over.
She was walking back to the hotel in a skein of mist,
and I slid out from the typewriter to read
a poem the color of her bare, luminous skin.

— II —

After André Rouveyre Fixes His Flat Tire They Will Drive to Deauville for the End of an Epoch

Apollinaire lifts his signature
bowler from his large Polish
head to the night in its caricature
of a starless sky, for roads taking one's soul
to other places always remain dark—and
beneath this epoch-ending first day
of war between Germany and France,
they will leave behind them
the swaying treetops, stars in their solar
ink, and the pure effect of art
as aphrodisiac visible in hay bales
no one will ever dream again.

Stillness is always this language
the poet can hear with the pebbles
talking among themselves
along the road when they walk
around like figures in a drawing
that have decided to leave the canvas.
André's wearing a bow tie, a short
and slender man like one's favorite waiter,
and on his knees struggles to repair
the tire's gaping puncture,
with his rubber gloves, unable
to draw upon any practical solution
except when it involves pen and paper.
The elbows of all the trees scrape one another
on this endless journey somewhere
they can never return from.

A moon has holed the midnight sky
and Guillaume wishes to drive their
automobile through that pale eye
watching him smoke a cigarette,
a man both Polish and Russian
who will enlist in the French infantry,
and stare up at the sky speckled
with phantom rockets.

And he will write to Madeleine,
a young woman met on the train,
how he wants to kiss her mouth
through her hat veil, a black pencil
working its spidery verse
on paper in one of those trenches.

André pumps air into the tire,
like gossamer the evening dew
wiped from his forehead
as he hears his friend with
his good taste in not objecting
to the flat tire and their delay home
talking about war as poetry
on their drive back to Paris.

Blood of Her Brother in Allegheny County, 1918

As she prepares for a day of scrubbing floors,
her brother who was gassed at the Battle
of the Somme with lethal chlorine will watch his niece,
as if from the sweetness of war came such beauty.
His lungs are clouds that never roll exalted
in a blue Prussian soul; his face is not for the future
despite the way he looks at an unswept floor.
Dear sister, he wants to say as she buttons
her linen dress up a neck that will never feel
her husband's lips lavish her with kisses:
There is hope in the smallest things.
But brained out with barbed wire and cannon balls,
he watches her bent shoulders stoop
to tie her black shoes muddied from melting snow.
He will never marry, and hacks like a saw
what's left of a conversation, hoisting one hand
above him for her to wait, then lowering
it to speak through his fingers that waggle
slowly he'll be alright. His coat bulges under the arms,
where threads are overstitched, and is loosely
dropped over a stiff high-backed chair, leaving him
almost a stranger in a crisp old shirt and suspenders.
There are many dead, he murmurs to himself,
thinking of her husband at three a.m.
not breathing, and is lost in thoughts
never departing or arriving in heaven,
but left somewhere in the outskirts.
Helpless among the living and the dead
from the gas still in his lungs, his palms spotty
with blood, he cannot love her any more than this,
staying behind to watch her child.

When Sergeant Reese Picks Up the Receiver

He sees the first October frost in the parking
lot, a hanging traffic light blinking
on and off as if in cardiac arrest,
and he looks at the scribbled phone
number on the back side of a matchbook.
He fought Sugar Baby in the warehouse ring
tonight, and his stomach hurt from the punches.
The boxer brandished his sweating gloves
above his head like Liston, and swore
he was going to leave him without front teeth
if he headbutted him again. But soldier boy
never did. He feels his front teeth, glad for them,
and wonders if he should call the blonde.
He inserts two quarters but changes his mind
suddenly, jams the phone back in its chrome holster.
He throws away the matchbook,
where she scribbled her number after he lost
and she followed him to his locker.
She said she looked good, if she wore lipstick,
puckering her lips into a smack, but he saw only
her badly dyed hair, and still saw it
though his sight had weakened in the scalding shower.
Inside the gym locker he left his bus ticket
to the base and another tour in Iraq.
The traffic light shakes in the wind,
as he remembers walking through a wall of punches.
Good for her. She got what she wanted,
to watch two men knock each other out.

Reese's Letter to a Son

I am looking at Saul Steinberg's drawings
for *The New Yorker*, the mysterious E standing
for what, existence? And as it rains here in California,
with you in Iraq, every splattering drop
brings me back to death. This suits my drawings,
the way I return to former lovers and never leave
their bodies, like your mother's hips in their tentative
walk, her breasts held in place by her hands.
Her black hair, the way it falls across her shoulders,
some freckles for bearings—her rising from bed for water.
Yes, her departing bottom, the lateness of our lust.
This suits my drawings of loops, not perfect circles,
for nothing is ever perfect. Even your mother's
heavy moods. My mind is both blurry and lucid
if I glance upward at the sky. I know you take
after your grandfather, who bathed outdoors
in a tub. There, in his soapy repose after days
on the road during the end of World War Two,
he paused for a photo. Grisly soldier with his helmet
on, cigar clenched in his mouth, as he displayed
a photo of John Wayne. I am drawing a nude woman
from memory, when she lay on her back, her knees
brought up to her chin. A process of erasure, yes,
not bothering to cover up any mistakes. You
are in Iraq, and dust blows over your head, as
you stride through the great Mesopotamian heat;
traffic on fire; and when you glance at women
in their flowing garments, I imagine you try
to penetrate their hijabs for their eyes, some part
of the female anatomy, even if only an elbow
thrown out a sleeve, a chin in its subtle beauty—
and I imagine you standing there, as the city burns,
trying to put all the parts together.

After the Saturday Night Fight Sergeant Reese Dreamed of the Blonde in Her Hijab

His nose couldn't be right, neither the helicopters
    in his head about to lower the patrol
into the neighborhood already blown apart
       by the Americans, and his taped fingers
    coming undone in their search for a nose—
drunk with Sugar Baby's blows to his face—
    like ground tromped by steel-toed boots,
and screaming helicopters remind him of Iraq

and the reader of Madame Bovary,
    her hijab aggressively showing a blonde curl
of her heresy—a woman barely twenty,
       and her fingers always on top
    of the American sergeant at a café table—
straightening his wild eyebrow hair
    or bending an earlobe closer before anyone
saw them looking into each other's eyes—

and he longed to say he loved that unnatural curl,
    despite remembering his father tell him
how his mother hated Marilyn Monroe, her curves
    leaving a crater in her head.
His letter told of some other bombshell in Paris, and the large
    dumb dog named after Marilyn was shot.
That pale bulb too much for his squinting slits, he fingered
    the broken teeth of his mouth, where Sugar Baby,
his opponent, knocked the hell out of his good looks.

Letters his grandfather wrote displayed in a mirror
    from the corners, small letters in cramped handwriting
almost Chinese, written upside down sometimes in foxholes—

he read them to learn more about love
and his habit of telling the truth. He waited for the doctor
        to inspect him like meat, tenderized by the fists
of Sugar Baby, after Reese called him a name he regretted
        in the clinch. He didn't know why he fought so many
rounds in that place they called Culture City.

A dirty old arena, and where is the culture
        in burnt-out neighborhoods? his head full of helicopters
going down in flames over dark yards where scrappers
                trespass for a dishonest living in Detroit
stealing copper. Reese on the mat heard the door click open
        for a doctor smoking a cigar, what a mess you are—
and Reese decided he'd marry his woman in the hijab
        who read Flaubert and waited for him in Baghdad,
if she still sat there, only daughter of a tailor who once sewed
                elegant suits, if Flaubert could reveal to her
a future with him, a rough American soldier who had watched
        her eyes that morning reveal everything she had ever seen.

Small Wanderings

Our fox who has graced us with his hunger,
whose instinct blooms among
the shadowy logs, selects food he can
hunt by his small black nose.
My wife with her burning black hair
leans through the opened window;
if she could she'd escape with him over
the fallen trees, the logs that
small animals use as highways.
Her fingers snap for his attention
where she has thrown sausage;
she wants to follow him to his den
dug out of soft, sandy soil.
Down into the warmth of the earth,
she will dream of a long hibernation.
Not as lost animals but ones
who survive a frost that can never
be kind when green tendrils
stand up to shout their silent death.
She wants to mother the fox
who offers his generous face of red fur.
An intelligence she observes
in his keen nose searching for fresh
morsels; a flicked tail of royalty
when it's time to run again
after staying too long under my wife's
hive of honeyed words. It is that red
fox face that knows more than
other animals within sight of people.
If you are lucky, the fox will reveal
through his gaze the soul's hidden places,
and you will take his broken trails
of the woods with you where you trespass,
an uneasy feeling when quick feet
barely grace the newly fallen snow.

Bridalveil Fall

There are moving shadows on the moon
that give no clues what anyone should do,
as spray vanishes in the air above Bridalveil Fall.
A soft glow of the endless teeth in the mountain
peak won't let us go. My wife's upturned face
reveals wrinkles around her eyes,
and she shivers beside me without a coat.
She remarks upon the moonrise, a hill where heaven
heaves out and the words echo in my heart.
Her gloveless fingers brush strands of gray
away from her cheekbones. She blushes
with a hidden thought, and I imagine
it flies off higher like a sparrow-hawk.
We have had our day of nursing rock paths,
roots like bone that we have traversed;
a photographic forever plunges us
further along the downward climb.
Touch was essential, throwing
away all perspective except that of fingers
on smooth stone, a handgrip
to pull us toward the clearing.
Every darkness can be backlit
with a kiss, stone in shadow
on one half while the other basks
in this burst light of the evening.
The moonglow over Bridalveil Fall
can never be forgotten, which will follow
us home as we think of oncoming night,
of what we could never reach.
Our lips intending to kiss but not yet,
like a vow we have to say as man and wife,
when words get in the way instead; words
husked until they're blown-away fluff.

Charley Kawbawgam as a Ghost Walks along the Presque Isle Path

Even the foam churning on the shore
in its whale splashes before returning

to the deep water, the massive desire
for an inward roaring, can't take away

this wonder of being alive. At the cliff
we hear the sibilant waves

on this wintry day come crashing
down in a drunken breath,

and accept we are one with loneliness,
one with a below-zero chill that bites.

Ten feet from the grave of Charley Kawbawgam
we brush the lines from our eyes,

stamp our feet to bring back blood
to our toes, and think of his roots

here on Presque Isle, where he lived
with his wife Charlotte and fished every day;

when he laid his ear to the earth
it trembled for the Chippewa man

and his auricula grew large, as if his ear
were able to hear everything.

Now Charley walks along fallen trees,
rock almost bleeding,

and hears Lake Superior dreaming
with strange wide eyes.

The Edmund Fitzgerald Is Out There

No sun today, the rolling choppers bent on their tempest,
and that great graveyard of water never
gives up its dead. A man beholds the suffering
in a flooding hatch, sees his fate suddenly sealed,
like Fortunato who recognizes the others,
the water an avalanche of cold that will suck out
your breath like the last minutes on a clock.
A ghostly bubbling echo of your remaining life,
hands struggling to remain above the waterline.
That's me in my tennis shoes, headed to the Coast Guard
Station, with its rescue vessel moored to the breakwall.
On the other side, wild water, and I always stop
like a sentinel to scan the heaving horizon
for a floundering swimmer, someone washed away.
It's this poem then with its slackening lines
that I'd throw to the drowning hopeless,
like those others falling into death's edge,
who happen to be reading my poetry,
deciding my syntax or subject, misplaced
commas: my name hardly mattering at all.

The Human Soul Is about the Weight of a Canoe

splashing under an unforgiving moon,
never able to find the right course,
more underwater than above, bucking prow seeking God
behind the bright blue lash of another wave,
like a soul ruffled inside out by a great northern wind.
The shivering Union soldier unballs his girl's letter
from his pocket, his neck roped in these veins
tying him to a chill, this gale blown up
from his dark soul, and his canoe with its ridged bottom
perched precariously on top of the waves.

Once ashore he'll sleep under a tree,
and want to reach under his lapis lazuli
for another letter of hers to read in the first snowstorm
and remember the wind-chilled spring
of men dying at Gettysburg. But his soul stretches
for miles over Superior's glowing milk-white surface.
All of the shimmering novas contain her name,
as the first flakes fly without a word of thanks
to her brother soldier at war, paddling
with a strange fear bristling at his neck.

She thought he had died and their baby
would be raised by a farmer who called her wife.
The chill bites colder as his canoe wobbles
through chopping rollers. His black-haired girl
Freda hates him because she's sure he died,
though he survived that winter to be more
than a soul blowing across a collapsed porch,
a fence torn out tooth after tooth, a rooster vane
whirling in the yard's rubble.

Let Me Make You Bloodless in a Single Flash

Don't breathe, the camera will not kill you,
the man says donning his shrouded cover

for a photograph of Bass Reeves, who feels darkness
sear skin just as much as the heat of the sun.

The starlight pouring forth in the constellation
catches him turning away to look

at the mountains, as if he were drawn
to something he can't ever get back,

like his slender wife with the name of Eulalie,
who died in his arms one winter night.

Now Bass wears a windblown straw hat
enslaving his brow in shadow,

his battered shoes bearing the weight
of a man who would never return home.

The former soldier, only nineteen years of age,
breathes through his bulbous nose

not knowing why he signed his name
on the form handed to him

with an immaculate white hand
by the fast talking Mathew Brady.

Time to go, his feet itching to move,
pick up his discarded rucksack

and walk until he can't see his steps
disappearing in the inky pools of no light.

A soldier who buried the Civil War dead
bounces a hand off his leg, whispering

how many souls are contained in a box
of your glass photographs:

bone, gristle and flesh gone,
he waits for a bullet that never comes.

Marilyn's Busty as Ever in Her Jean Jacket on Location for the Making of *The Misfits*

Pyramid Lake, Nevada, 1960

The cowboy's dog, Dooley, restless
on his leash, bites the hand
of Marilyn who attempted to feed it
a morsel, smelling animals about to die.
Hawks circle above in a cloudless sky
over the flatbed's shadow;
and cowboys too old for Hollywood
see ghosts drift off the mountains.
At first her character Roslyn won't know
the mustangs are for pet food,
not pets for children, as the cowboys
jabber to dismiss their before-scene jitters.
She stands alone to the world,
the boom mic finally holding out its filter
over fine dust, her eyes flashing
she missed her chance for love;
her white hair across her brow
like some confession when a photographer
catches her before the shot dense
with hot blood, something unforeseen
about to knock her down, her fists
pumping against her dusty jeans.
And if she could go home she would,
but first her tits must shout to the mountains.

General Johnston's Love for the Fallen Soldiers

For the dead who lay strewn on the bloodied earth
of Shiloh, the bodies beneath a blue-eyed sky

that never changed sides, Confederate soldiers
slain along with their Union brothers

overbalanced unexpectedly by musket balls,
legs severed in a blast, let me sing your song

at Shiloh Church, near the Tennessee River,
Hardin County. I was one of you, a man whose artery

spurted blood, toppled from his horse,
an officer who heard your love songs

reduced to murmurs; all of you pleaded
to be alive, crawling like a tortoise toward me

whose heart beats madly to hold you all in.
Beneath a crimson sun cannons echo

their cacophony. Let me live one more day
to scribe letters to my beloved, bulging

pockets with words to tell of love's insistence,
to whisper early in the morning campfire

those lies to my soldiers who believed each wrong
was right, and the right was good enough

to march upon blue-bellied men whom
at Shiloh Church we caught by surprise.

The Kitchen

Ghostly smoke, the first cigarette of the day.
It was my mother's idea to smoke only there,
where she could usher open the door
and let the fire inside a cigarette
burn its ash elsewhere besides her son's lungs.
Her eyes already swallowing the day
that would never get better,
despite her starlet appearance.

Smoke empties out in sorrow
out of that kitchen, and through
the screen door mesh outdoors.
A cigarette extinguished in an ashtray
that burns for years it seems
after leaving that room.

John Keats One Evening Beheld Lake Superior

When we turned over in our dreams
we found each other standing there together,
not in lone splendor but her hand in mine;
it was like John Keats had unraveled his breath
speaking of his first touch of a woman.
Keats had checked in at the hotel and lived
down the hall with Fanny, coughing
but laughing in her arms, or so I imagined
blue-eyed Fanny, with her bare shoulders,
and her undying love at the Old Marquette Inn,
where one could see through a window
the bright canopy of clouds over Lake Superior.
Keats mumbled something about nature's gentle
doings, but there was nothing gentle about the waves
that destroy boats like the Edmund Fitzgerald.
It was a dream after all, and I imagined John Keats
telling his Fanny it was all right. But he had tuberculosis
and it would never be right between them in bed,
coughing blood into both cupped hands.
His hair tousled like an old mossy hill, he begged her
to lay down, all arms and legs as she undressed,
but would he ever be man enough for her?
Keats pensively looked out the window at the stars.
He could dream of his life ending in bed with her,
of the soul's pleasures, how a warm jet of blood
escapes through the arteries, his own love for her
tightly rooted in his chest, if he could only breathe,
touch any part of her now, and like all dreams
they end before they have begun.

Billy the Kid's Been Shot

Love kept him alive for days
on his saddle. Inside the gunfighter,
this filament of light. Under him
his horse-hobbled gait.
Dizzy arc of buzzards overhead.
His death ride may kill him
or reunite him with Angela.
Staring up at the stars, their prickled
cluster of no return, he feels his lips bead for mercy.
In the heat of the desert lavender hair tonic
crosses the corner of his mouth—death lurks
above as a hawk, or shadows that eat up
gaping rattlesnake holes. It's so hot
and he wishes to return, the sand dune
lying there, her body. He's William Bonney,
shot and sand-blasted. He knows he's wanted:
Pat Garrett sworn to bring him back over the saddle
of a horse from Mescalero Territory.
He talks crazy, seeing Angela's hanging braids,
as if she were with him on the horse,
her breasts against his shoulders.
He now gets what death is, with his wound
seeping through his shirt. A tortoise
like a stopped clock lifts its ancient head
to watch a grisly, unshaven face,
dust whipping up, his teeth clenched
with sand that's ingrained against sunburned skin.
When he removes his hat, it blows away
from him like a lost thought never to reclaim.

Window

A snowy owl on the fence post
eyes her through the thick-paned glass

as if it knew her melancholy
had always been knotted to this night.

Its head rotates in a circle
as if dissatisfied with what it sees

and her perspective of a muddy road
frightens her, as she peers out

from a Missouri farmhouse
at that other knot—horse riders.

Suddenly, the owl in soulful hoots
warns all living creatures of its power

and a gray field mouse is frozen
in a puddle beneath the fence post.

She touches death up around her neck,
almost out of breath, and a noose of hair

loose over her bare shoulders as she trembles,
worrying about the children upstairs.

Her mouth hurts from those prayers
grasped like a hand ripping a dress—that

fabric of faith splitting at the seams
bunched up and tossed.

A night for murder, mutters the owl whose
body—compact and dangerous—descends;

any low-flying tree branch will do
for a hanging if they catch Jesse

for the trains and stolen horses,
their voices aimed at Zerelda,

any fleeting shadow outside,
like the hoary visage of winter

with unfolded wings as it swoops
away in the moonlight and her head reels,

thinking of her floor to be disgraced
by the ragged resolve of boots.

— III —

Sleeping Woman

Walt Whitman closes his eyes and remembers
the dead from the Civil War, too many bodies
that he touched under the billowing canopy
of the field hospital after their battle.
When his forest gray hair falls across
his wrinkled wren of a nose, his scar above
the mouth wants to take wing from names
he can no longer pronounce. He stumbles
with his head swimming with their faces
toward the cot where he sees a sleeping woman.
His reddened eyes from no sleep stare down
at her shiny black hair, as she shifts a full-blown
breath in her unbuttoned nurse's top.
He wonders at her breasts peeping from
the loose clothes, her own way of thinking
through her nipples. The old poet grasps
his beard as if words were hiding there.
The sleeping woman recognizes him,
the poet who writes of the human body
in its many forms, not that she doesn't
like seeing a man or woman naked,
but she brushes these thoughts away.
Whitman rocks back on his heels,
asking for heaven, but suddenly
collapses to her cot, almost pushing
her off. Lord help me, he intones
to her bare chest, her eyelids fluttering
like a dragonfly uncertain where to land.
Her knees meet her chin halfway,
seeing the wound-dresser stagger and gasp
his breath as if it too was a battlefield.

Jim Harrison Walks Out for His Mail

He wears an open shirt anxious
about the mail the postal lady fed
his metal box on this below-zero morning.
Sometimes he meets his mail carrier
to talk about her body, how she's grown
beautiful, like an orchid with her blonde hair
unfazed by the graying strands.
His one eye peers up at the angry clouds
rolling in from Lake Superior.
She deserted him in a hurry, sending
snow flying up from her tires
down the lonesome road where people die.
Harrison, the old dog of a writer,
idles with his diabetes, bursitis, and bad dreams.
The last star of the evening bends its light
upon him, like some forgotten canvas
of a man named Van Gogh, he thinks,
who loved to chew on paint chips
and envision crows assaulting him
in his trek across a wheat field.
Now his words are coming back
in an oversized manila envelope.
Like Van Gogh, he shipped off his soul
to somebody who would judge him.
His balls ache from the cold,
because he's not wearing underwear
and vows never to change anything.

Mescalero Territory

His fever grew used to the soft light
in the barn, where rats were leaving

a string of marks on his arm;
the room he sensed was the place to die in.

A bullet in his belly, still his dreams
rose with him in the night's rafters.

He missed Paulita Maxwell's body,
out on the moonlit porch of his desire,

his outlaw kisses riding across her neck,
down through the valley of her legs.

He wanted to be Billy the Kid
in every word he said, his greasy voice

speaking to those bloated rats
eating their way toward judgment.

The last man he shot was Bob Olinger,
sad sonofabitch jailer who'd mocked him

as young Billy. "Hey Bob," Billy shouted
back from his escape, aimed the shotgun,

and blew Olinger's head off and rode away
on his stolen horse into Mescalero Territory.

Now, in the long cool shadows of the granary,
Billy felt the ground barreling away

out from under him when he stood up,
lifted one foot off the floor, and scooped up oats,

feeding his mouth, as if it were a cathedral,
to bless himself with bloody hands.

Honey Drinkers

If you don't believe in slow motion
there's no reason for you to listen
to the fingerprints of their flutter,
or watch their bills collect honey
from the feeder as if the world
were standing still. They leave
it exactly where it was when
they hum somewhere else,
you disbelieving you have seen
them at all, as you watch your wife
close the balcony door. Inside, her bra
is unaccounted for and her nude
body becomes this way to picture
heaven as she looks for her clothes.
A fleeting, ephemeral moment,
as you are left hanging in air
like a honey drinker in the drizzle
that morning decides to sprinkle
upon you shirtless and humming.

We Didn't Know the Teepee Would Catch Fire

His daughter asleep in the backseat
had his eyes and would forget these nights
when she didn't know who her father was.
We neared his farm in the Keweenaw,
and tonight we would present her to him.
I wondered who my child would look like,
if I ever had one, but this child wasn't mine.
When we found his farm, I didn't want to see
the bed where his daughter was conceived.
His friends surrounded us, and a lone spire
of smoke traveled up into the starlit cold;
our visit lapsed into a party, which
included his original girlfriend.
Mine with her unquenchable heart sat beside me.
I helped her give birth a year ago,
the midwife watching as I cut the cord.
Her long brown hair unwrapped like a scarf falling
over her shoulders, such broad ones,
as she handed her daughter to the bearded father.
If I glanced over to my lover, it hurt thinking
her honeyed loins was what he coveted
on that one long weekend away from me.
The annunciation came not from angels,
but drunken words of sleeping alone,
waiting for her return, even though I reflected
"the only people for me are the mad ones,"
which Kerouac once said in conversation.
The tall, bearded farmer said we could sleep
in the middle of a snowy field, where his teepee
stood erect, if we were able to get a fire going.
Under all those stars, smoke rose to a chalked sky.
The canvas flaps caught fire; we ran naked

under a ghostly moon, my cock flopping.
We escaped to sit on frozen seats,
hoped the engine would groan.
We prayed for someone to forgive everything,
but never knew who that could possibly be.

Cold Snap

I wonder why cold has to snap; fingers
can barely move when frozen, hoping to unlock
the getaway car from the tundra of a parking lot.
Temperature signs advertise our downfall:
five degrees below zero. I imagine the whole world
sinking like the Bismarck into frigid Atlantic waves.
My favorite film as a ten-year-old, slouching
in sticky seats below a barrage of small candy.
All those pre-teens in a throwing frenzy.
Our only radar system was to duck as we settled
down to watch. Death proved too interesting
to ignore; the prime minister in his porcelain lisp
said those famous words, "We must sink the Bismarck."
That super fortress blew the guts from British cruisers;
an uneasy stillness stuck to us, like the cold
in my later years. I won't mention my age
or where I am watching the time and thermometer,
except it's at McDonald's and I have no job.
They price the coffee at the current temperature
when it falls so far. They owe me many nickels
for this week of the Arctic chill. Walking around,
we have no idea when the cold will unsnap,
like some rubber band at the other end of winter.
I stare at slow-moving vehicles covered in permafrost.
Then snap my fingers. I am unemployed,
and my wife tells me to leave the house
and nothing about my feeling of helplessness.
Work is a dream chariot, and you wait
for a job that never comes; back at home,
faucet leaks keep up this steady beat.
But I sit here with a pencil, pad of paper.
I know words are ghosts; they reappear

on the page after you erase them.
Let their smudges speak to us, even this snap;
the burning cold of us seated at a table,
where we whisper work is salvation.

Good Night, Dr. Caligari

The snowplow lights our room by the window.
My wife slips off her nightgown, shivers
in the glow. Her black hair whispers
across her back and before my hands know
where to go, our arms and legs tangle.
We fling our hearts into a silent film.
We're singing when the doctor appears
at the bed, wearing yellow trousers
creased like envelopes. She bites my lips,
not afraid of those movie characters, faces
once ten feet tall on the screen, who step
out of my head, roll their eyes at us.

When Dr. Caligari tips his hat, out spills
a shock of white hair, like desire itself;
his huge face fades into this one single thing
as he walks through a wall, embarrassed
to see my wife. Her sleek white body
crouches over my root, and the snowplow
rattles the teeth of my typewriter.

Picture how we scald our cheeks against the heart's
furnace, the snowplow lighting up our room
as if it were heaven, our stubborn love
allowing Dr. Caligari to return with a silence
that's cinematic as he kneels beside our bed,
empty even of any somnambulists.

On the Day of the Armistice in Paris

Apollinaire smokes a cigar, the silk
of clouds torn apart and crudely roiled
like one of Picabia's paintings
with ruddy earth-tone colored planes.
His bowler set upon his knee in the Tuileries,
he watches a woman wearing tight leather
shoes bend over to pull up a garter
as if showing off to him more leg
with its black stocking than necessary.

His head belongs to a Greek statue,
his heart maybe this chipped stone
and he remembers dizzy headlights
for eyes as they drove down a lime-covered
road headed nowhere but to the trenches.
Rising from where he sat, he taps
his fingers on the bench and walks away
across grass with a jagged scar
on his skull from shrapnel.

Dear Gui, one of his letters from Madeleine
addressed him, the girl on the train to Nice
whose mouth he kissed through black lace.
Most of her letters burned in his dugout
after he was assaulted with mustard gas.
This scrap has survived, but he can't read
the rest, and dizziness like staring down
from the Eiffel Tower shoots behind
his pain-blasted eyes until he can't walk.

The poet whose mother was both Russian
and French draws upon an imponderable breath,
searching for his true identity but only
finds he has fallen to the wet grass of the garden.
His burning cigar gone, and his one hand
raised for no reason at all, he lies there still
and watches her breasts exploding above
into shrapnel with the pointillist stars.

At the Lonely Café Poe Is Back from Nevermore

The collar of his wrinkled shirt up around
his bird neck, he sits at a table
behind you, his back always against the wall
like Wild Bill. Edgar Allan Poe dressed in black,
his mustache unwieldy, his voice flying
when he implores his strange bird of unhappiness
to depart, telling it where to go,
as you crack the spine of your book of poetry
even louder to disappear in disquiet—
your lonely café reading time disturbed.

His shoulders bear that weary bird
of Lenore singing. And he does his best to cry
for the waitress with red hair, his coffee cup
empty, but she ignores the man from Baltimore,
as if he were last night's drink that set her hangover.
If only he'd stop staring at you sunken
in disappointments, those photographs
of melting ice that was clearly your soul
only another poet could see.

You carry his poetry in your pocket
when you go out the door in a bewildered gaze.
Snow falls out of a kindness to cover up
the ugliness in everything like old album covers.
You touch your open-necked shirt and tightly pegged trousers;
your fingernails are dirty from digging your own grave.
His eyes show miles of madness walked
for heart chords never played.

He calls you by name, your nose hair bristles.
You smell that nevermore
when you scrape back your chair to escape.
You don't move as that ancient weary bird
looks at you straight, in your hallucination

that will take pills to mend.
All the coffee drunk that morning
making you nervous, you imagine a raven
rustling its wings, whispering that one word
of Lenore, as you trudge home through the snow.

Long After the War

John Lennon was dead, the radio voice in French
  almost weeping, and Reese thought about the bathtub
in Munich he had shared with the *Vogue* correspondent,
    Lee Miller—Hitler's love nest rooted out during
the waning days of war. Reese piled up their armor and helmets,
  the Kodak in his other hand, and Lee said shoot the picture.
She wanted to be a famous photographer, but was all arms

and legs in the tub. She was his dark spool of thread
  sewing the war years together. He saw her
face on magazine stands, and often compared her to Bella,
    his thirty-year-old lover. The old veteran who never
abandoned Paris slept with women years younger,
    and he felt young again, in his underwear and desperate beard—
his boy and wife back home dead to him.

But the radio wouldn't play any jazz that night.
  Monk was gone, so was Miles Davis and his holy
trumpet. He'd go downstairs right now to the record store
    down the block and buy all the jazz he loved.
His Paris girl was slightly more drunk than Reese.
  He loved to see her smeared blood on the toilet seat.
Look at this, he'd say, you are alive and could have children,

and she laughed when she sat atop his lap,
    her hair with its bobby pins coming undone,
falling to the floor and swimming with the leftover bottles:
    his weathered bridge of a face where displeasure
often crossed his squinting myopic eyes, the corners
    of his mouth holding onto words he shouldn't have said.
Now John Lennon was dead and he was surrendering

his comfortably bare feet to shoes, without socks,
    to hell with them, and Bella was crying
because she had loved Lennon. But she couldn't say
    why, in her Italian house dress, her wildly blonde hair
with its split ends spilling across bare shoulders,
    but told him don't leave me, baby.
And he heard that December wind shaking his shutters;

standing up without socks on, Iowa returned to him
    with the moon slanting cold into the snow,
the coyote wandering out there in the frozen field,
    making his voice known. He saw the inside
of the barn where he had tarped his roadster
    and kissed its chrome fender for luck
when he was drafted by the army and good as dead.

She set it ablaze, he learned, in one of her
    nearly illegible letters wishing him dead.
Late-night drinking and womanizing helped him forget
    all about Iowa; headphones on,
he traveled everywhere through music, until she meant nothing
    to him—and Bill Evans on piano did.
He wondered why he had ever married her.

He cursed Lennon, throwing up his arms,
    and was on his way out, much to the chagrin
of his god of selfishness—long after the war he vowed
    never to care about anybody but himself—
all of his friends and lovers had died—and he tripped
    down the stairs to street level and the night
devoured him in its icy blast, his voice howling.

He was in the wrong place without a coat,
    no socks and his eyes misty behind a pair

of slightly bent wire-rims, out in the open where he walked
    hunched over as an old man remembering
the rocket flares overhead and the groaning artillery,
    and how he had to reach the dying
to carry them back to their foxhole.

All around him he heard John Lennon singing,
    but he cried instead for himself, his sheepdog murdered
in a cornfield by his wife—the crowd sang to be part
        of history on the street corner, where they waved
their American friend closer—he wanted defiantly
    to tell them in his own bitter voice
he never needed anybody's help in any way.

The Last Place on Earth in Mexico City

The fix-it guy wearing a faded eggshell-colored
cap cracks his melody maker from its case
to play his high-pitched teardrop of a note.
Everything I do is to improve the sound,
Francisco mutters with a cigarette chumped
down on his lower lip, wheezing more
of his accordion that he's repairing today
between his sunspotted hands of sixty.
His eyes are of the night without sleep,
blowing leaves across an empty plaza,
forlorn calls of his empty stomach
as his fingers try to burst open a melody.
His slender figure of a man who's still in his prime
leans his cheek a certain way that tells
of a woman not yet forgotten, as his eyes roll back
in this lost tango loved by Jewish Iraqis
and Arab orchestras. His hips torn one way
while the rest of his body complains that
it can't follow his feet on such an unimportant morning
as this, the whiskey bottle full enough on a table
beside broken accordions like his Excelsior,
white as a snowy owl that roosts on the floor.
But Francisco suddenly stops as if seeing death
in the corner of his Mexico City music repair shop,
those buskers and maestros of an exhausted earth
on their way to the graveyard despite
little resurrections made by men like him.

Robbie Robertson Sipping a Bitter Coffee while Bob Dylan Types His Next Song

We are dying every day;
those clouds rose from her dark hair
when he was a boy and his Jewish father's
body was uncovered from the metal of a crash.

Next room, Dylan dances across
an old typewriter, and drums of the reservation
like Robbie's heartbeat ache
for everything to go away, his mother
a Mohawk who breathes through
his eyelids for him to hear those early songs
learned from the ghosts who walked
through the midnight drums.

Every morning he mops up sad-eyed
eggs he chased around the plate, and sees
his mother combing her long black hair,
as if every chord he'd ever play
had her fingers in it.

At Big Pink, the holes in the floor
leak the basement tapes trapped on reels,
the piano down there with its funny yellow teeth,
the drum set ready for radio—both
of them prophets, Robbie at the kitchen table,
a cigarette dangling from a lower lip,
as he hears Dylan slam back the carriage
as if still traveling in a Buick
with worn-out brakes and windows
rolled down for anything that goes by
on America's billboards fading into history.

Nothing left but grounds in his cup,
Robbie's fortune rides far and wide those Southern ruins
of his gothic muse, smoke pouring
from his mouth like cotton fields aflame.

Dylan strips the wrinkled page
from the platen and stands up, his cigarette
teeth-clenched, and shouts, "We are going
down in the flood," and Richard Manuel,
in his bear-like shadow, leans toward
the first step of the basement, behind Levon
in country short hair of a farmer
who's dreaming of his next crop.

Before Robbie sets down
his coffee cup, he looks outside at the crows
in their clothesline straight flight
into the huddled trees, Danko
striding out of them wearing his Billy
the Kid hat atop bushy hair,
as if he were coming straight from
a shootout, and again in his heartbeat,
restless sleep of a weight Robbie
can't ever lift, prays his mother to
forgive him for these guitar licks
and smoke that drifts without any words
like a religion he chords every dying day
in the biting steel strings of his Telecaster.

Blue Raincoat

Leonard Cohen never showed himself
around a corner, but kept himself in cafés
with songs on the tongue of his hoarse voice,
bleary windows holding the women
who answered to Jane and were nobody's wives.
I lost myself on Saint Catherine Street,
bleeding words that kept me much older
than I was at twenty-four.
My own Jane slept in a tourist room
above a shoe store with her daughter
after we had walked almost the entire length
of Old Montreal to dine at the Polish café
where the waitress spilled water onto my lap.
Wiping, she spoke with her dark bangs
adrift across her forehead, and her
tight flower-patterned dress, her knees bruised
and nearly bloody from scrubbing floors.
"Tell her you love her before you eat a single bite."
Her words crossing the round tablecloth
of several coffees and red borscht
from another world to my lover's bemused
expression. Then soon a sad blessing
when she said I was younger than a father
should be but father to the daughter
who sat there barely three, and
who would never recall this French scene.
The girl loved me, though, her father
not her father, and the waitress
removed her washcloth from my lap, asking
if it felt good. Outside in the rain I wasn't
wearing a blue raincoat torn at the shoulder,
and as much as I wanted him here,
it got darker when I thought of him stealing
my woman with his gypsy looks,
and L. Cohen wasn't anywhere to be seen.

In My Sleep a Vague Gray Shape of a Wolf

turns solid when like Zhivago I wipe a space
to see through a frosted window
a wolf not a hundred yards away.
But headed in my Irish cap
down Sunset Boulevard, no wolf at all,
a short-haired German shepherd
stands guard in the Scientology lot.
Fever of sentences sends me to the poem
that will form under my fingertips
where wolves wait in their hunger,
that Urals hideaway known as Varykino
when I was fifteen years old.
On the balls of my feet, a much younger
man today, here in Los Angeles,
at the year's beginning, its funnel of ghosts,
the heart's valve opening and closing,
as I return to Zhivago wiping away
the frost on the window.
For I have left my love sleeping,
like he has Larissa Fyodorovna,
no longer a boy who saw a brother poet
in cinemascope one wintry evening.
It is my hand rubbing the image of a wolf
clearly enough to be seen through the window's frost.
A lean wolf with his bones of a shipwreck,
his soulful eyes like ink we use
to write poetry, larger than any
of the wolves who want to eat us, our blood
already spilling from his eyelids.

A Radio with Guts

Bukowski talked about it, the one he threw
through the window each drunken night
and it still played, a radio indestructible
with songs that couldn't help but bead
against my forehead. I think of Johnny Rivers,
honeyed in his tenor and hair, the way
he sweetened even "Secret Agent Man."
Edgar Allan Poe sat with Bukowski
throughout those drinking sessions.
Whatever he poured down his gullet had
to burn like being tied to a stake, when
the Raven began talking Plutonian shores.
As a young man I remember summer
nights of cheap vodka, descending
with a friend to the cellar, where
we waited out the dawn to burst
into song in my yard. With first rays
we moaned like Cat Stevens. My father
still alive and younger than I am now,
we swirled our vodka with heavy cream,
as we headed off, trying to learn how
to become men; the radio with its guts
removed on my father's bench, wiring
to be rewound, tubes to be replaced.
Here was the Philco that reposed
on its shelf, one that Bukowski might
have thrown through his window,
all in its magnificence of old parts;
a radio that never worked my whole childhood,
though father would disappear down the stairs
to putter with its guts to make it sing.

After the Bars Closed Cars Would Line Up for Gas

At the last pump, in a sports car
without any headlights on,
a young couple kisses, the girl's blouse
opened for him on the last day of summer,
radio on playing the Eagles.
I can't help but look at her mouth
barely breathing with her bra
off her shoulders, as if it's too late to change
what is going to happen in a hurry
where he'll spread out a Hudson Bay blanket
for her hips to lay in the grass.
The neon sign of the station
illumines my fingers, as I flash
my rag over their filthy screen.
Much clotted mud on the side by the door,
too, but that's not my job, after they
swerved wildly alongside a pump.

I stand over a boiling radiator,
visible to them but not seen as they kiss.
Late at night, when anything can unfold
after drinking, I dream of my lover asleep
in her valley of a soft bed beside her daughter.
The busty breezes keep me awake.
It'd take me ten minutes to walk home,
but I am working till daybreak.
I search their engine for its dipstick,
a flashlight aimed close to its heart,
when I locate the carburetor, leaning
closer, my body nearly swallowed
by all those belts. I peer in, with the girl
watching me, holding the stick

that wobbles in the wind,
the other cars honking for service
because I'm taking too long,
straining to see more of her body.

Her knees perched up, in the bucket seat,
her shapely thighs almost ghostly
in their glow. And the car line out into the street,
their last chance at gas before home,
doesn't disturb me. The dipstick is there
to touch, and with the flashlight clenched
between my sternum and neck,
I check the oil on it with my fingers
first, unsure of the level, wiping
the dipstick clean, the girl's face
showing worry that I have seen
too much and looking ashamed
now of my presence, as if the world
was riding on that thin greasy line.

In Just about Two Minutes Jack Kerouac

hallelujahs to the seagulls
when he drinks down each coffee.

The Indian waitress whose name is Lenore
offers Des Moines, Dubuque, in her refills.

His thumb extended like a hitching post where ravens
fly down to roost and squawk.

A jukebox dime plays North Platte
coming on fast as the boy rolls across America

and the waitress pirouettes Kearney,
Julesburg, Cheyenne in her dark hair

when she delivers his breakfast on a tray
and he pictures Four Corners when she drags

a cigarette from her left brown ear, his bill
slapped down like Kansas City.

Look at young Kerouac with a shirt his mother
ironed before he left the house

roll on from his own Lowell with his country
pack full of Boston, farms and rivers.

The boy knows he's always departing in his smile,
or arriving somewhere else with a sigh.

Salt Lake City he spins around on his stool,
hears giggling girls at a table from him.

But the midnight blue of a moon-soaked cloud
over Mariposa leaves Kerouac alone

on the diner stool, his hair dark
as a night gone on the road.

In a Field Frozen over in a Mining Town

These boys of recovery gather sticks
to bend in a wild slapshot
across the bare-knuckled ice.
They love the sound of a ricocheting
puck, as their skates tear up
their lives in perfect circles:
no homes, parents who don't want them
hoping they will disappear out
a window and never return.
They hear the poor box of the church
cracking open with their crowbar,
Jesus crucified in the dark
watching them turn and run.
Every time they hear a bad muffler
they cringe for their own truck
that broke down when they were arrested.
They pull on three pairs of socks,
wooly beasts that eat them up,
fidgeting fingers busy when they
lean down to lace their skates, as if this
is the only thing they will ever know.
The ice is calling them: danger,
addiction, loose-limbed bodies,
hair flying over shoulders,
once they invite the ice to crack
under their speeding skates.
They watch me working
as the friendly prison guard,
their substitute teacher.
If they breathe too hard, ice freezes
on their nose. They shout mostly
at each other, hear their voices

carry across the mining town's rink.
Nobody complains about the cold.
Their next high they shouldn't think of,
but the sound of ice under their skates
reminds them of that grinding crack,
and mothers addicted and living
in their station wagons may be just
driving by right where a boy aims
his slapshot, drives his puck.

Opening a Door to Deliver a Newspaper

A paper rolled up like a baton
to drop behind an icy door, after
hearing the hinges complain.
Something in his step buckles
as he scuffs across the sidewalk,
a shadow of himself walking.
Now everywhere he sees the winter
cold as his brother. The lawns dark
with dreams like furniture
left out all night in the snow.
He's old enough to complain
about everything, his wife
on the side street, black hair dangling
over her back, an unshoveled porch,
a small slot she jams a paper into
and nearly falls as she steps down
off the undisturbed snow.
His block takes an hour to zigzag
house to house, the world fallen
around him in whiteness.
He suspects his wife walking
the next block has the figure
of Sophia Loren and a face
that scares him with its beauty.
The frost sticks his tennis shoes
to the sidewalk, so he hurries without
seeing if his own shadow follows,
his Irish cap doffed to show no hair.
They look at each other but
not knowing what to say go their
separate ways; he kicks snow
with the leaves, discovering they

are the color of blood, as he watches
his shadow disappears, part of himself
left standing. What he wants is to collapse
in bed with her, so he can memorize
her curves, hook his fingers over
the plastic band of her panties
and draw her close.

— IV —

Looking for the Road to Verona

Her shades back on, the sun splinters
into varied hues. No words pass between us:
we hear our tires meet the gravel,
those words almost spoken,
for they are better as secrets
only two people share.

There's lunar belligerence
in that August moon aglow
while we search for the right road
beneath a field's slow fade over.
Startled night birds rise
from the strange writing on golden
curls of blowing leaves.

Gray pockets of driving at dusk make me
want to touch the graying hair behind her ear.
A hand sharing a bag of chips with her
longs to explore everywhere,
something intimate but in such
a simple way as drawing the back
of that hand across her cheek.

Her blueish-gray eyes filter into mine.
The darkening fields are littered with our fears
for an older couple, who want to catch
another holy moment in bed.
But the road leaves us with its birds
in flight over the moon's face,
bothered by obtrusive clouds.

No signs tell us anything of Verona
where we must turn to find our son's
road, and both of us look out
for the deer who slowly
cross the road like pilgrims.

The House Was Full of People All the Time and Maybe Too Much of Billy the Kid

was blowing through my head and maybe
a flat region with no trees; cactus wheels

rolling out of nowhere; a man can't live
until he dies was what I thought,

as my winter chair creaked that morning,
and I expected to hear distant gunshots

in Mescalero Territory. And I imagined Billy
waking up with Angie; he couldn't have been lonesome

if he tried, her hip a mountain when he unloosed
himself to climb down from that moon they rode

together each night. I wondered if he thought
about dying. When I rose from my chair

she came closer, her soul unbuttoned
like her dress. I thought about Billy again,

his buck teeth glistening, that Irish boy
from New York, outlaw at the drop of a saucer

or some ghost of a knock at the door.
And as she bent her face into my neck,

sensing we were coming too close,
I remembered his hand trick in capturing red flies,

the way Billy practiced to stay alive,
to avoid that sugary mess, spilling guts

after being shot. She said Billy won't mind,
and I hooked my hand behind her neck

for a second, as if nothing mattered
but this celerity in her sudden kiss

on my cheek and how Billy could blow you apart
with his six gun in the sun or dark.

King John

We crowd into a room sound-proofed with concrete,
  dreams heavy as metal sometimes.
I face down the piano's white and black keys, hoping
    for them to take me past
the jagged edges, but under my hands
  they go their own broken-toothed way.
We are working up "King John" for the late John

Renbourn, guitarist who died at the Scottish border
  in his converted church—twenty guitars and four
turntables, in dust, beside the pastrami
    and cheese left on the cutting board.
King John drove miles in his Rover from this remote sanctuary,
  and rode back through the night,
if he could, after concerts, but one day he never showed

up for his gig. Renbourn once was a young guitarist,
  dangling cigarette from his lips and his maze
of acoustic notes bewildered the moon
    as much as his guitar companion,
Bert Jansch, who had to find the notes
  as fast as he could play them. Young, my bandmates and I
hauled its grunting weight out to the garage.

We gathered where farm rakes and shovels lined the walls,
  the ruined Triumph station wagon center stage
without its engine, hung outside on hooks almost levitating
    like our sound, on hooks in the air, the gasp
of a Les Paul breathed through a Leslie speaker. We'd haunt our songs
  like young wizards. Like Led Zeppelin at Olympia Stadium,
that dazzling bowed guitar of Page, ripping through silence

like a freight train—stunning as Robert Plant sang
   "Dazed and Confused," a sound that made my ears
into bells ringing for an hour after the show. But that riff's gone
   replaced by King John, silver haired and overweight,
who'd never tell us what happened to him that night
   he never showed, but somehow we found him in our chords alive
head collapsed on the steering wheel, his engine running.

His Motorcycle Crash Started It All Over Again

That day I'm singing to "This Wheel's on Fire,"
the one the boys buried in the Basement Tapes,
with Robbie's Telecaster and Dylan singing about losing control.
It resonates deeply since losing my job and starting over,
at least something like that, the same you could
say for Rick Danko and Richard Manuel,
tripped down from their wild tour days
to over-easy eggs and cigarettes in the kitchen.
No auditorium of thousands. Just starting over,
with endless cups of coffee, waiting for Dylan
to settle behind the microphone again,
who wants to sing "Tears of Rage," its melody
written by Manuel, but doesn't since he can never
come close to Richard's high notes.
The boys on the payroll now, since they were his
tour band, and none of them had jobs.
Dylan reaching for "Too Much of Nothing,"
a song that he just pulls out of his pocket
on a badly typed crumpled sheet.
How Elliot Landy caught them beginning all over
in the Big Pink basement, in his wide-eyed photographs.
Bobby wearing a coonskin hat, Manuel consorting
with a mandolin, stretched out on a bed.
Outside a lens idling over Levon sitting
on a Cadillac hood, its front chrome
teeth knocked in from crashing
a guardrail along the mountainside.
Or them on a bench, grouped
like a disaster about to happen, staring
at the woods as if a bear were emerging.
One day Dylan crashed his motorcycle,
that metal grinding on Striebel Road.

His sharecropped hair buzzed short now, wisps of a beard
and vinegar voice, which he'd never planned on
singing, trying to get something straight, probably
moving sideways down the road anyway.

Richard Brautigan Appears at the Gas Station One Night with His Girlfriend

He's wearing the same tall big-brimmed hat
on the cover of *Trout Fishing in America*,
and his hands slide off the steering wheel
of his jalopy so he can gesture to you,
in your faded red sweatshirt, your own oil-stained
poet mind, for what in hell does Brautigan
have to do with the Upper Peninsula?
You pry open the hood of his car, a pump jockey
under bug-stained lights, no longer nineteen
and in love with every word he's written,
as if his hippie girlfriend in those knee-length boots
doesn't mean any more than a late-night customer.
She marches quickly inside, past your sentinel
of a chair, the greased-up paperback, where you have been
reading *Trout Fishing in America* to the blinking neon.
Brautigan mentions his engine's overheating;
and he might as well have said General Lee
was staying down the street at the local hotel,
many of his men hopelessly alive in their wheelchair
graves. But his teeth are talking, the poet
who once stood before Ben Franklin's statue,
in his tightly worn vest with goddess beads
dangling between the lost buttons.
And you want to tell him he needs a can
of oil, dipstick in your hand, beckoning
before they can drive off to find one more
unmarked road leading nowhere into the night.
But by then the hippie girl in her tight-fitting boots
goose steps by you. Her great white wrinkled skirt
of many hours drags across the oily bay,
as she whispers, "See you later, alligator."

Poe's Hat

Not that he needs a top hat
to prowl around Baltimore bitten
by a rabid dog, a mad hound
he perhaps wanted to bewitch
behind the barrels of stinking fish guts.
But his offered hand to comfort
any snarling commentary resulted
in gashed fingers on his right hand.
He'd never play the flute for weeks,
not that he'd pick up his fluttering
without the dead girl he loved
who dueted with him on flute
on any wild, stormy Plutonian night.
If he survived the madness
or was found like a black cat
on top of one of those barrels
raving about his young bride,
whose nipples he entertained
with his midnight black mustache,
he'd pour himself a deep bath
to lay down his dreams in,
watching his toes submarine
from the frothy milk-white water.
He forgot what he was doing
in Baltimore, white linen coat
and black vest, his top hat
with the broadest brim sometimes
like his grin sprouting in terror
of living alone, that brim bent
in recognition of ravens tumbling
from his tempest, one Raven stopping
to quote Nevermore to the Black Cat

Poet, his hands plunged into caverns,
all of his soul a flirt and flutter to shadows.
His immediate task was to crawl toward
the midnight bone of an unholy street.
Darkness there and nothing more.

I Return to the Surface of the Earth Wearing
My Miner's Helmet with Its Third Eye

November 3, 1926

searching for the men who killed me
who said it was safe to work below
swampy ground on that November day
of the Barnes-Hecker Mine disaster.
As a working man I learned Italian
from the sons of immigrants, my tongue
a shovel and hammer against that rock
of silence we're digging underground.
The mine disaster left my wife a widow,
a young woman of nineteen from Norway,
who wore a flapper's hat shaped like a helmet
and shook the parlor's soul when she danced.

Let me rise and breathe in the cold,
gooselike as a ghost circle chimney smoke
straggling from homes. I was the last man
in the mine to die, to moan my wife's name,
to see her round face and golden-brown hair
before breath made slaves of us wanting
air before our death in November.
We expected snow over muddy ground,
children to whoop and yell for lost souls
on All Hallows' Eve, for a sea beast to surface
from Lake Superior's gray choppy foam,
for the witch to ride her beanpole
through the chill and cut a silhouette
beside a hungry moon: one day of the year
for those souls to construct a show.

If you see me in my miner's helmet,
boots with untied laces, susurrate
a surprised prayer, for my third eye searches
for the men who killed me,
those owners who might be washing
their hands of the dead, the men who are
preparing for sleep by stepping into

flannel. Don't listen to the ghostly
creaks of our phantom weight,
tiptoeing forever the same steps
around their beds, we, the dead,
can't escape making sounds
as we haunt a house. A carbide
lamp's flame from a helmet
flickering upon a wall and our presence
lasts as long as a bad dream when
those bosses find a new sleep position
with a belly flop and cry out names
from the troubles in this world.

I want to remember what it felt
like to be a man with my wife,
watching her toil at English, words
as big as her eyes looking at a son
of a Swedish immigrant, soup warmed
up that afternoon, for me to work
and return home, not expect women
buried in shawls and their revolution
of red eyes. They said it was safe
for fifty-one miners underground,
the deluge of the tunnel
not possible, but our last bulwark
was our big shoulders floating
under broken timber and rock.

Inside Tumbleweed

All the butterflies you have
ever seen yellow

contained in its desert glow
before you walk away

to a tumble yourself,
a place where

moonlight shines
on old bones—

past the forlorn metal
crossed in railroad tracks

and a coyote panting
for an invisible waterhole.

Of the white dust
that belongs to no one,

you grab a handful
in the kneeling down

and won't give it
back, and see your son

spread his camera
stand for starlight—

a stranger in the desert
who touches the stars

in their desolate orbit
fat in their milky way.

The road you are
striding along is a river

current of brown sand,
and you bend your head

almost in prayer, beading
words said to someone you loved.

Your old bones rolled
past sorrows

as you get
so small inside

tumbleweed,
without anywhere to go

you vanish—
hungry,

your hat full of tumble-
weed, it seems,

and stars that never
empty from your brow.

Jack Nicholson and His Horribly Wrong Grin

His hand lost in the popcorn bowl,
he told his maid-slash-girlfriend,
in Coco Chanel perfume and little else,
there must be a better life. She spiked
the kitchen floor in high heels,
poured another lover in her martini
that she'd sip down to an olive-green gaze;
she heard Jack growl the lines he spoke
years ago in *Blood and Wine*: "Sometimes
you got to keep up relationships." Testing
that memory, his belly peeking out of his shirt,
his chops found the cadence: "Baby, you're
killing me with those brown eyes."
Pissing in the bathroom, he stood estranged
from his younger self, his surprised old cock
wondering about women. On that road
one drove through Death Valley, hair tonic
the only drinking water after a point.
In his failing air conditioner there was no hope.
He stared back at the actor who regarded
good days gone in the mirror. His hair plugs
were desperados on the run; his dreams
drank for him these days, so many drinks
he couldn't remember their names.
This left his eyebrows jumping around
as if in conversation, his beard wisped from a week
of not shaving, and sideburns rugged from
a part he played where he hated everyone.
But that was years ago and he saw Maria purse
the pearl necklace he bought for her, making him
think back on *Blood and Wine*, the housemaid
played by Jennifer Lopez who helped him in the heist.

"I'm going to take you places, baby," he told her,
but his girlfriend's rattling the keys to his Mercedes.
His hair plugs gone to the desert without him.

Lifetime Spent as a Beatle Stranded
on a Couch before a Television

John Lennon, naked, holds in a melody
he has to smoke out, till he understands
why he got so old at seventy.
His heart beats rapidly, perspiration
on his skin, remembering how large
his heart was that night of his near death,
and screams Beatle cadences from "Twist and Shout."

Without all the bones of winter dug up,
he hooks that crooked trademark nose
to Central Park, and sees himself walking below.
Through the blustery drifts he looks down
at his assassin hiding in the shadows,
waiting for a second chance to kill him,
for all the bullets missed his heart
the first time, in spite of it being huge
as a cathedral that night standing
in the cold outside the Dakota.

He mumbles to the television
not turned on, his heart wants to be big again,
fearless with an engineer in a studio
cutting new songs, and to hear it beat
unashamedly for a woman—he doesn't care
who it is. And like a rock star about to get a hit,
he turns his back to the window, let it be now,
one more bullet to send him up the charts.

Snowy Owl

In the afternoon of our errands,
we took time to drive behind the store
and look for the snowy owl
on the electric lines, as if this power
painted his feathers the color
of a moonrise over the water,
a thick smooth silver when he lifts
his wings to feather down
on an unsuspecting mouse; my wife
told me he'd be waiting here,
in his territory, as if his talons already
were charging up for his prey.
If we could talk to the owl,
we could have asked him
about his home, if it was true
he had flown from the Arctic,
leaving behind the ice's shifting bones.
When an owl's feathers are as snowy
as winter, she still knows
the menace of its talons.
Her cheeks begin to clam,
thinking how she likes to talk
to the animals, and if we were closer
he would have spun around
his fantastic movable head,
looked into our eyes for those secrets
we could never hide.

Rick Danko's Last Song

Danko settles in, a slow one that arches
his back so somewhere in the chords
there's stage fright and nowhere to hide.
Nobody notices he's out of tune.
As a child he listened to Nashville
on a dusty wind-up Victrola
and played his seesaw fiddle
that traveled the rails on his strings
to every loose place he imagined.

The night he ran away he wore
a borrowed leather coat with patches
on the elbows in southwest Ontario
to join Ronnie Hawkins' rockabilly band.
He sang in dank barns as a teen
creating a slow boiling rhythm
with his hands on a mandolin, his voice
of Appalachia pitched high for notes
brought down from the mountain.

Now Danko knows the teeth of the wind
biting the antenna of his camper
as he balances between lines all night
and closes his set at the folk club,
his heart already miles ahead, dialing
in all the fences that await like heaven
for him. The ex-member of The Band
tells those who gathered his CDs for sale,
his big face splitting a smile.

He slides his three hundred pounds
from his stool. His last song trails off,

his heart riddled with holes he can't repair,
his slow steps meeting the floor, as applause
leaks through the crowd's thin fingers,
their hands making such a noise
when he turns to say goodbye.
Fame's like a sudden river he must swim,
as he walks out the door.

A Polish Professor Tells Me I Am Wearing the Same Kind of Hat as Czesław Miłosz Years Ago

For a short moment there is no death.
Despite the expanse of nothingness that is Lake
Superior a few blocks away. Time does not unreel
like skein and the horizon may be only a wheel
turning over dappled clouds, and look the beer's
pithy as winter psalms. Words are what we are truly
wearing, seated outside under a glowering mixed-up sky.
A Polish professor with the build of a boxer, a mind
of wiper blades clearing any cluttered ideas from his sight,
jokingly mentions we are having a good time
up north away from the diploma factory.
I am a wanderer who happened by to say hello
to a friend from Wales, and I have joined
these good men for a beer and I am wearing a floppy fedora
that the Polish professor reminds me was the hat
Miłosz wore—and I am glad for that—for anything
tonight on my way up the street to another bar.
But why not sit awhile and talk about Czesław,
whom I met in the back room of a café
where he demolished a whitefish and drowned
in a carafe of burgundy? Now, he said, pushing himself
back in his chair, let's talk. And we did.
Like we're talking now, candidly, in the telescope's
eye of a watching someone and that may be God
or not. Czesław was friends with the pope,
and they wrote letters back and forth in their larger
remaining years in Kraków. Piotr, the professor,
buzzes with ardor for life, Sławomir Mrożek,
the playwright who wrote so many unusual plays.
I feel my years fade away as one does drinking

beer, and everything seems to be an endless wedding—
of youth and age—trying to gauge any rain later;
and the metal chair seems comfortable for now,
the beer affording us time to talk like fools
and not mean it, the way up the street postponed,
the uncanny chill about to fall brightened by our lively banter.

Billy the Kid in a Bookshop

Poetry was as dangerous as his fast gun.
He'd shoot it out with Federico Lorca
when he carried his books into the desert.
They'd find him even with Ferlinghetti's work,
out among leftover stars before morning.
The blonde cashier asked him if he was famous.
But Billy thought only of Boot Hill
and the 400 graves left unattended.
The gunslinger was paging furiously
through a Bible he kept in his top pocket
of his chapped jean jacket, a ranch hand
who caught straying cattle for John Tunstall,
an English rancher who taught the Regulators
croquet before he was murdered. Billy the Kid,
lost in time, found his fast draw was for books.
He should be in a desert hole, not here,
visible to his killers. He hadn't shaved in three days.
"You look kind of familiar to me," she whispered,
mistaking him for someone she could not name.
There seemed to be an uneasy truce between him
and the world of poetry. Her freckles danced
when she asked if she could snap his picture for their wall,
and without making a foolish move he smiled back,
his buck teeth like the dull blaze of bullets.

Notes

Long Upper Peninsula bus rides were rites of passage, and I had many of them during cold winters when it wasn't advisable to hitchhike. Boarding one of these bus rides, I happened to notice a prisoner just paroled being dropped off at the station by a guard. We rode for hours in a crowded bus. At our first stop in the middle of nowhere, I followed him into a convenience store. I strolled with him under the bright neon on his first night of freedom. This was how "Break from the Bus Ride: Convenience Store on US-2" was written and became a poem for January in *Writing after Roethke: 12 Months of New Poetry Inspired by Theodore Roethke and the Roethke Poetry Prize.*

"Sergeant Reese Pummels Sugar Baby in the Ring" imagines a soldier on home leave boxing. He will have to return to Iraq but boxes Sugar Baby in the ring. He is battered by Sugar Baby and his friend Kojak drinks with him later in a bar where Reese can't stop talking about a Muslim girl he met in Baghdad. I like to think of Sergeant Reese as a character in a film I am writing, seeing his swollen face like a Steve McQueen character or even a younger Tom Waits, whose gravel voice can't be silenced after drinking Manhattans. This character will return to Iraq and die in a firefight, but I can hear his voice talking in the bar in Detroit.

"Something about Eighteen and Goose Lake Festival Where I Saw the Flying Burrito Brothers Play" recalls that time of the Vietnam War and the draft. Death was a reality for a boy of eighteen. Goose Lake Festival seemed to be a turning point in my life after I barely escaped being drafted. I was going to live. On television boys my age were coming home in body bags. At the festival I saw Ten Years After and Mountain as well as Detroit bands like Third Power and The Stooges. In that mix was the Flying Burrito Brothers, with that strange name and Gram Parsons singing most of the vocals.

Apollinaire, drawn by Picasso, has his iconic bowler and bow tie like a smile that never seems to come undone. He wears the uniform of the French infantry where he got shrapnel in the head from German artillery shells. His *Calligrammes* are magical drawings that display secret zones of the body. Desire is a phantom rocket bursting above the trenches. A cannon aimed at the enemy becomes a woman's rump. Apollinaire with his large head of Russian and Polish ancestry is my muse. One of the first poets whose worldly voice caught my attention as a young man in his twenties. I leave a place for him in each of my poetry collections. They are my signature: that widely expressed cursive of my soul and manhood. Here in this poem, "After André Rouveyre Fixes His Flat Tire They Will Drive to Deauville for the End of an Epoch," we see Apollinaire, the poet, about to join the French artillery.

A recurring character for me is the Civil War soldier hoping to heal himself from what he has seen in battles like

Gettysburg. He canoes through windswept waves along the Lake Superior shoreline. He ponders his soul and how heavy it weighs. "The Human Soul Is about the Weight of a Canoe" is my poem's title and his answer to his soul's weight. There is another heaviness here as well, and it's the thought of his girl wedded to an old farmer. It will be him who raises the young soldier's child.

———————

Minié balls were invented for maximum human damage. They were cylindro-conoidal bullets that could shatter bone and result in amputation. The round balls tended to remain lodged in flesh. In the Mojave Desert death became an addiction for some, and a black gravedigger was asked to pose for a Mathew Brady photograph. He was told the camera would not kill you, but he didn't believe that. "Let Me Make You Bloodless in a Single Flash" was a lie. A photograph was as lethal as a bullet in portraying human damage.

———————

It was not hard to imagine John Keats living at the old hotel up on the hill. He wrote about things of beauty, and through a window overlooking Lake Superior he saw the marbled waves in motion and the whitecaps trying to flee their fate. The hotel was where I wrote love poems for my girlfriend on a manual typewriter. I thought about John Keats in a room down the hall with his girl Fanny and the noise they made making love. In our room we disturbed Mr. Marshall next door, a stylish elderly man who ate out every night. John Keats would have found the hotel as a last chance for love before he died of tuberculosis. "John Keats One Evening Beheld Lake Superior," and so did we as lovers who lived there for a short time. We used a hot plate that blew fuses, kept our milk out on the window ledge.

"Billy the Kid's Been Shot" imagines the desperate escape of William Bonney from Pat Garrett, known assassin and once a friend to Billy. The dizzy arc of buzzards overhead foreshadows what will happen to Billy in the end. But death has been pushed aside and he has to fight off the buzzards and hunger. Time is like a stopped clock of a tortoise in the Mojave Desert. He thinks of women, talking crazy to himself about a certain girl named Angela riding naked with him in his saddle.

"Jim Harrison Walks Out for His Mail" dreams of the writer in mystical terms, as if he has grown larger than any poem. He peers up at angry clouds rolling in from Lake Superior. The last star of his night's drunken feast with a seven-course meal hangs low in the sky. Harrison dreams of the sky as a canvas that Vincent van Gogh once touched with the expressive colors of his soul. It is here at Harrison's Grand Marais residence where we find our own balls are aching from the cold.

Another recurring character is Robbie Robertson of The Band. He plays guitar at Big Pink with Bob Dylan who rattles his manual typewriter in the kitchen before songs. There are photographs that document this house and what was created musically in the Basement Tapes. They show the young musicians wide eyed and eager to make anything happen between cups of coffee and cigarettes. Bob Dylan in short hair of a farmer sits at his manual typewriter like Dylan Thomas sucking on a cigarette hoping to create art. Robbie's Telecaster is his typewriter: he's chronicling his Mohawk and Jewish roots, and the ghosts from those midnight drums who appear to never settle. In a few months Big Pink music will make them famous. "Robbie Robertson Sipping a Bitter Coffee while Bob Dylan Types His Next Song" lays down these narrative bones of a feast about to be eaten.

"Blue Raincoat" comes from a visit to Montreal with my girlfriend and her daughter. Up and down Saint Catherine Street we walked with her daughter in a stroller. We kept expecting Leonard Cohen to appear somewhere in Old Montreal, but he never appeared. One night I went to a strip club with Carlos, the fellow we met on the Canadian train who told us where we could stay in rental rooms above a shoe store in the business district. Carlos and I were supposed to pick up his wife at one of the strip clubs where she was working. I had made the mistake of drinking too much. In an alcoholic stupor I sat down at a crowded, smoky cafeteria, where a fried egg sandwich nourished me enough to return to the subway line, late for the Chinese meal we had planned on our last night in Montreal. Certainly what I had seen at the strip club would always stay with me. A young dancer expressively showed her body to us while Joe Cocker's song, "You Are So Beautiful," played. The way she raised her arms and lowered them to the music, letting us see her breasts beneath her long black hair falling with her pointed nipples, was beautiful.

I was young and working the night shift at a gas station. My lover lived down the street and I would return to her at seven in the morning. But those nights alone were full of fish flies blown in from Lake Superior and lonely travelers. I read voraciously when I had the chance to sit down in a metal chair outside the station. One of those books was Louis-Ferdinand Céline's *Journey to the End of the Night*, and if I pick it up today I can see the greasy fingerprints left there when I was a young man in love. "After the Bars Closed Cars Would Line Up for Gas" attempts to remember the silence and the fish flies as well as learning how to live in this world.

"The House Was Full of People All the Time and Maybe Too Much of Billy the Kid" comes from reading Michael Ondaatje's *The Collected Works of Billy the Kid*. Often I sat at the local library either reading or working up poems on the computer; one afternoon a woman with her children arrived and recognized me as the poet who put her into one of my books of poems. She came over and bent down to kiss me on the cheek. In the poem she kisses me on the lips. She said more that I can't express here in words. I was thinking about Billy the Kid capturing flies with a quick hand, how he kept his hand skills ready to draw down on a man with his six gun.

Edgar Allan Poe is my dark muse. The night he grew sick from a dog bite and possible rabies, he wandered Baltimore in his distinctive stovepipe hat. I wonder what he really did that night when he went mad. Who recognized him in the backstreets and minor roads of his feverish imagination? What poetry did he scribble down and ball up and throw away for a hobo to pick up and read? "Poe's Hat" bears all of this in mind as he suffers and dies. Maybe I am deathly afraid of dog bites myself, after being bitten by Mr. Bouchard's standard poodle as a child in my neighborhood. Bouchard kept walking on, his poodle off the leash, and a cigar in his mouth.

"Inside Tumbleweed" was written while walking in the deep fine sand of the Kelso Dunes at the Mojave National Preserve. In my floppy sunhat I felt like a naturalist or Walt Whitman ready to write a poem of an exuberant experience observing sand the color of bone. There were traces of small animal prints, squiggly lines at times, or barely anything at all for the eye to see. The sand blew away and came back from the mountains, as if God were writing his own poem for us to read.

Acknowledgments

The author wishes to acknowledge the following publishers of the poems in:

The Big Smoke America: "Richard Brautigan Appears at the Gas Station One Night with His Girlfriend" and "Lifetime Spent as a Beatle Stranded on a Couch before a Television"

The Briar Cliff Review: "Blue Raincoat" and "Bridalveil Fall"

Capsule Stories: "Small Wanderings"

Cobalt Review: "Willie Horton Dressed in his Baseball Uniform, after Playing the Yankees at Tiger Stadium"

Dunes Review: "Drinking with Jim Harrison at the Hotel Bar," "Charley Kawbawgam as a Ghost Walks along the Presque Isle Path," "Honey Drinkers," and "The Last Place on Earth in Mexico City"

Flyover Country: "Looking for the Road to Verona," "Window," and "The Human Soul Is about the Weight of a Canoe"

Hiram Poetry Review: "*They Really Make a Mess Outta You*"

I-70 Review: "A Last Picnic"

Michigan State University Libraries Short Édition: "Richard Manuel Crashes His Cadillac," "The Edmund Fitzgerald Is Out There," and "Dead Poets Who Visit Jim Harrison"

North Dakota Quarterly: "When We Lived at the Old Hotel"

Plainsongs: "Something about Eighteen and Goose Lake Festival Where I Saw the Flying Burrito Brothers Play"

Acknowledgments

RESPECT: The Poetry of Detroit Music (Michigan State University Press): "On the Bus Downtown along Woodward Avenue the Driver Turns around to Say They Killed Marvin Gaye"

San Pedro River Review: "Love Song with Boreal Forest" and "Inside Tumbleweed"

The Seventh Quarry Poetry: "Blood of Her Brother in Allegheny County, 1918," "The Kitchen," "Wandering the Yellow Dog," "In Just about Two Minutes Jack Kerouac," and "Billy the Kid in the Lava Tube"

The Shore: "Let Me Make You Bloodless in a Single Flash"

Slant: A Journal of Poetry: "Sleeping Woman" and "On the Day of the Armistice in Paris"

Sou'wester: "Reese's Letter to a Son"

Speckled Trout Review: "Billy the Kid's Been Shot" and "Billy the Kid in a Bookshop"

Streetlight Magazine: "A Radio with Guts"

Superior Voyage: Marquette Poets Circle (Gordon Publications): "Cold Snap," "My Dreams Never Caught Their Bus," and "Marilyn's Busty as Ever in Her Jean Jacket on Location for the Making of *The Misfits*"

Twyckenham Notes: "After the Saturday Night Fight Sergeant Reese Dreamed of the Blonde in Her Hijab" and "A Polish Professor Tells Me I Am Wearing the Same Kind of Hat as Czesław Miłosz Years Ago"

Undocumented: Great Lakes Poets Laureate on Social Justice (Michigan State University Press): "I Return to the Surface of the Earth Wearing My Miner's Helmet with Its Third Eye"

Visiting Bob: Poems Inspired by the Life and Work of Bob Dylan (New Rivers Press): "Robbie Robertson Sipping a Bitter Coffee while Bob Dylan Types His Next Song"

Whimsical Poet: "Lost: A Love Poem for Emily" and "The Sweet Loneliness of Solitary Travel"

Acknowledgments

Writing after Roethke: 12 Months of New Poetry Inspired by Theodore Roethke and the Roethke Poetry Prize: "Break from the Bus Ride: Convenience Store on US-2"

"Billy the Kid in the Lava Tube," "Billy the Kid's Been Shot," "Inside Tumbleweed," "A Last Picnic," and "Marilyn's Busty as Ever in Her Jean Jacket on Location for the Making of *The Misfits*" were written during a Mojave National Preserve Residency.

This book wouldn't exist without the amazing heart and mind of Dr. Ross Tangedal. Let me heartily thank him and his dedicated Cornerstone crew who touched my words and made them into a book to admire. Brett Hill was the first to work on my book, and I felt his care for language in his careful scrutiny of my words. But the others—Ellie Atkinson, Carolyn Czerwinski, Zoie Dinehart, Kirsten Faulkner, Natalie Reiter, Lauren Rudesill, and Anthony Thiel—were believers in the ultimate poetic expression, too: a new book of poetry, mine. I felt this profoundly when reading their comments for the poems included here in *Let It Be Told in a Single Breath*.

I would also like to thank Peter Markus for his ability to locate the heart of a poem, my illustrious editor for *Father, Tell Me I Have Not Aged* and Marick Press, and Jonathan Johnson for his secret Scottish soul headed to a glen with my poems in his backpack. I also couldn't have done any of this without Rodney Torreson's keen eye and heart. In addition to these poets, much gratitude goes to the creative forces behind the following musicians: Dylan Trost, whose Americana chords opened up roads for me; Jeremy Morelock, whose soundscapes allowed me to write of other earthly, eclectic places; Cal Freeman, whose electric ear caught the innermost secrets of my words; Greg Ormson, for the half-dozen outlaw songs he forged from poems; and Steven Curtin, for his electronic compositions that made my words electric.

Russell Thorburn is the author of several poetry collections, including *Somewhere We'll Leave the World* (2017). A National Endowment for the Arts recipient and first poet laureate of Michigan's Upper Peninsula, he lives in Marquette with his wife. His poems have appeared in many literary journals and anthologies, including *RESPECT: The Poetry of Detroit Music, North Dakota Quarterly, Dunes Review,* and *Sou'wester.*